ALBERT CAMUS

The Fall

The Fall

A Novel by

ALBERT CAMUS

TRANSLATED BY JUSTIN O'BRIEN

Some were dreadfully insulted, and quite seriously, to have held up as a model such an immoral character as *A Hero of Our Time*; others shrewdly noticed that the author had portrayed himself and his acquaintances. ... *A Hero of Our Time*, gentlemen, is in fact a portrait, but not of an individual; it is the aggregate of the vices of our whole generation in their fullest expression.

—LERMONTOV

B K CLASSICS
An imprint of B K Publications Private Limited

Published by

BK CLASSICS
An imprint of **B.K. Publications Private Limited**
967/2393, Shiva Nagar, Tankapani Road
Bhubaneswar – 751018, Odisha, India
Tel: +91 674 2971856, 2433856, 2430238
Email: info@bkpublication.in
facebook.com/bkpublications
twitter.com/bkpublication

The Fall

Albert Camus

Reprint, 2024

ISBN: 978-81-19348-27-5

Printed and bound in India

Contents

About the Author

Albert Camus was born in Mondovi, Algeria, in 1913. After winning a degree in philosophy, he worked at various jobs, ending up in journalism. In the thirties he ran a theatrical company, and during the war was active in the French Resistance, editing an important underground paper, Combat. Among his major works are four widely praised works of fiction, *The Stranger* (1946), *The Plague* (1948), *The Fall* (1957), and *Exile and the Kingdom* (1958); a volume of plays, *Caligula and Three Other Plays* (1958); and two books of philosophical essays, *The Rebel* (1954) and *The Myth of Sisyphus* (1955), both of which are available in the Vintage series. Albert Camus was awarded the Nobel Prize for Literature in 1957. He was killed in an automobile accident on January 4, 1960.

I

May I, monsieur, offer my services without running the risk of intruding? I fear you may not be able to make yourself understood by the worthy ape who presides over the fate of this establishment. In fact, he speaks nothing but Dutch. Unless you authorize me to plead your case, he will not guess that you want gin. There, I dare hope he understood me; that nod must mean that he yields to my arguments. He is taking steps; indeed, he is making haste with prudent deliberation. You are lucky; he didn't grunt. When he refuses to serve someone, he merely grunts. No one insists. Being master of one's moods is the privilege of the larger animals. Now I shall withdraw, monsieur, happy to have been of help to you. Thank you; I'd accept if I were sure of not being a nuisance. You are too kind. Then I shall bring my glass over beside yours.

You are right. His silence is deafening. It's the silence of the primeval forest, heavy with threats. At times I am amazed by his obstinacy in snubbing civilized languages. His business consists in entertaining sailors of all nationalities in this Amsterdam bar, which for that matter he named—no one knows why—*Mexico City*. With such duties wouldn't you think there might be some fear that his ignorance would be awkward? Fancy the Cro-Magnon man lodged in the Tower of Babel! He would certainly feel out of his element. Yet this one is not aware of his exile; he goes his own sweet way and nothing touches him. One of the rare sentences I have ever heard from his mouth proclaimed that you could take it or leave it. What did one have to take or leave? Doubtless our friend himself. I confess I am drawn by such creatures who are all of a piece. Anyone who has considerably meditated on man, by profession or vocation, is led to feel nostalgia for the primates. They at least don't have any ulterior motives.

Our host, to tell the truth, has some, although he harbors them deep within him. As a result of not understanding what is said in his presence, he has adopted a distrustful disposition. Whence that look of touchy dignity as if he at least suspected that all is not perfect among men. That disposition makes it less easy to discuss anything with him that does not concern his business. Notice, for instance, on the back wall above his head that empty rectangle marking the place where a picture has been taken down. Indeed, there *was* a picture there, and a particularly interesting one, a real masterpiece. Well, I was present when the master of the house received it and when he gave it up. In both cases he did so with the same distrust, after weeks of rumination. In that regard you must admit that society has somewhat spoiled the frank simplicity of his nature.

Mind you, I am not judging him. I consider his distrust justified and should be inclined to share it if, as you see, my communicative nature were not opposed to this. I am talkative, alas, and make friends easily. Although I know how to keep my distance, I seize any and every opportunity. When I used to live in France, were I to meet an intelligent man I immediately sought his company. If that be foolish ... Ah, I see you smile at that use of the subjunctive. I confess my weakness for that mood and for fine speech in general. A weakness that I criticize in myself, believe me. I am well aware that an addiction to silk underwear does not necessarily imply that one's feet are dirty. Nonetheless, style, like sheer silk, too often hides eczema. My consolation is to tell myself that, after all, those who murder the language are not pure either. Why yes, let's have another gin.

Are you staying long in Amsterdam? A beautiful city, isn't it? Fascinating? There's an adjective I haven't heard in some time. Not since leaving Paris, in fact, years ago. But the heart has its own memory and I have forgotten nothing of our beautiful capital, nor of its quays. Paris is a real *trompel'œil*, a magnificent stage-setting inhabited by four million silhouettes. Nearly five million at the last census? Why, they must have multiplied. And that wouldn't surprise me. It always seemed to me that our fellow citizens had two passions: ideas and fornication. Without rhyme or reason, so to speak. Still, let us take care not to condemn them; they are not the only ones, for all Europe is in the same boat. I sometimes think of what future historians will say of us. A single sentence will suffice for modern man: he fornicated and read the papers. After that vigorous definition, the subject will be, if I may say so, exhausted.

Oh, not the Dutch; they are much less modern! They have time—just look at them. What do they do? Well, these gentlemen over here live off the labors of those ladies over there. All of them, moreover, both male and female, are very middle-class creatures who have come here, as usual, out of mythomania or stupidity. Through too much or too little imagination, in short. From time to time, these gentlemen indulge in a little knife or revolver play, but don't get the idea that they're keen on it. Their role calls for it, that's all, and they are dying of fright as they shoot it out.

Nevertheless, I find them more moral than the others, those who kill in the bosom of the family by attrition. Haven't you noticed that our society is organized for this kind of liquidation? You have heard, of course, of those tiny fish in the rivers of Brazil that attack the unwary swimmer by thousands and with swift little nibbles clean him up in a few minutes, leaving only an immaculate skeleton? Well, that's what their organization is. "Do you want a good clean life? Like everybody else?" You say yes, of course. How can one say no? "O.K. You'll be cleaned up. Here's a job, a family, and organized leisure activities." And the little teeth attack the flesh, right down to the bone. But I am unjust. I shouldn't say *their* organization. It is *ours*, after all: it's a question of which will clean up the other.

Here is our gin at last. To your prosperity. Yes, the ape opened his mouth to call me doctor. In these countries everyone is a doctor, or a professor. They like showing respect, out of kindness and out of modesty. Among them, at least, spitefulness is not a national institution. Besides, I am not a doctor. If you want to know, I was a lawyer before coming here. Now, I am a judge-penitent.

But allow me to introduce myself: Jean-Baptiste Clamence, at your service. Pleased to know you. You are in business, no doubt? In a way? Excellent reply! Judicious too: in all things we are merely "in a way." Now, allow me to play the detective. You are my age in a way, with the sophisticated eye of the man in his forties who has seen everything, in a way; you are well dressed in a way, that is as people are in our country; and your hands are smooth. Hence a bourgeois, in a way! But a cultured bourgeois! Smiling at the use of the subjunctive, in fact, proves your culture twice over because you recognize it to begin with and then because you feel superior to it. Lastly, I amuse you. And be it said without vanity, this implies in you a certain open-mindedness. Consequently you are in a way ... But no matter. Professions interest me less than sects. Allow me to ask you two questions and don't answer if you consider them indiscreet. Do you have any possessions? Some? Good. Have you shared them with the poor? No? Then you are what I call a Sadducee. If you are not familiar with the Scriptures, I admit that this won't help you. But it does help you? So you know the Scriptures? Decidedly, you interest me.

As for me ... Well, judge for yourself. By my stature, my shoulders, and this face that I have often been told was shy, I rather look like a rugby player, don't I? But if I am judged by my conversation I have to be granted a little subtlety. The camel that provided the hair for my overcoat was probably mangy; yet my nails are manicured. I, too, am sophisticated, and yet I confide in you without caution on the sole basis of your looks. Finally, despite my good manners and my fine speech, I frequent sailors' bars in the Zeedijk. Come on, give up. My profession is double, that's all, like the human being. I have already told you, I am a judge-penitent. Only one thing is simple in my case: I possess nothing. Yes, I was rich. No, I shared nothing with the poor. What does that prove? That I, too, was a Sadducee ... Oh, do you hear the foghorns in the harbor? There'll be fog tonight on the Zuider Zee.

You're leaving already? Forgive me for having perhaps detained you. No, I beg you; I won't let you pay. I am at home at *Mexico City* and have been particularly pleased to receive you here. I shall certainly be here tomorrow, as I am every evening, and I shall be pleased to accept your invitation. Your way back? ... Well ... But if you don't have any objection, the easiest thing would be for me to accompany you as far as the harbor. Thence, by going around the Jewish quarter you'll find those fine avenues with their parade of streetcars full of flowers and thundering sounds. Your hotel is on one of them, the Damrak. You first, please. I live in the Jewish quarter or what was called so until our Hitlerian brethren made room. What a cleanup! Seventy-five thousand Jews deported or assassinated; that's real vacuum-cleaning. I admire that diligence, that methodical patience! When one has no character one has to apply a method. Here it did wonders incontrovertibly, and I am living on the site of one of the greatest crimes in history. Perhaps that's what helps me to understand the ape and his distrust. Thus I can struggle against my natural inclination carrying me toward fraternizing. When I see a new face, something in me sounds the alarm. "Slow! Danger!" Even when the attraction is strongest, I am on my guard.

Do you know that in my little village, during a punitive operation, a German officer courteously asked an old woman to please choose which of her two sons would be shot as a hostage? Choose!— can you imagine that? That one? No, this one. And see him go. Let's not dwell on it, but believe me, *monsieur*, any surprise is possible. I knew a pure heart who rejected distrust. He was a pacifist and libertarian and loved all humanity and the animals with an equal love. An exceptional soul, that's certain. Well, during the last wars of religion in Europe he had retired to the country. He had written on his threshold: "Wherever you come from, come in and be welcome." Who do you think answered that noble invitation? The militia, who made themselves at home and disemboweled him.

Oh pardon, *madame!* But she didn't understand a word of it anyway. All these people, eh? out so late despite this rain which hasn't let up for days. Fortunately there is gin, the sole glimmer of light in this darkness. Do you feel the golden, copper-colored light it kindles in you? I like walking through the city of an evening in the warmth of gin. I walk for nights on end, I dream or talk to myself interminably. Yes, like this evening—and I fear making your head swim somewhat. Thank you, you are most courteous. But it's the overflow; as soon as I open my mouth, sentences start to flow. Besides, this country inspires me. I like these people swarming on the sidewalks, wedged into a little space of houses and canals, hemmed in by fogs, cold lands, and the sea steaming like a wet wash. I like them, for they are double. They are here and elsewhere.

Yes, indeed! From hearing their heavy tread on the damp pavement, from seeing them move heavily between their shops full of gilded herrings and jewels the color of dead leaves, you probably think they are here this evening? You are like everybody else; you take these good people for a tribe of syndics and merchants counting their gold crowns with their chances of eternal life, whose only lyricism consists in occasionally, without doffing their broad-brimmed hats, taking anatomy lessons? You are wrong. They walk along with us, to be sure, and yet see where their heads are: in that fog compounded of neon, gin, and mint emanating from the shop signs above them. Holland is a dream, *monsieur*, a dream of gold and smoke—smokier by day, more gilded by night. And night and day that dream is peopled with Lohengrins like these, dreamily riding their black bicycles with high handle-bars, funereal swans constantly drifting throughout the whole land, around the seas, along the canals. Their heads in their copper-colored clouds, they dream; they cycle in circles; they pray, somnambulists in the fog's gilded incense; they have ceased to be here. They have gone thousands of miles away, toward Java, the distant isle. They pray to those grimacing gods of Indonesia with which they have decorated all their shop-windows and which at this moment are floating aimlessly above us before alighting, like sumptuous monkeys, on the signs and stepped roofs to remind these homesick colonials that Holland is not only the Europe of merchants but also the sea, the sea that leads to Cipango and to those islands where men die mad and happy.

But I am letting myself go! I am pleading a case! Forgive me. Habit, monsieur, vocation, also the desire to make you fully understand this city, and the heart of things! For we are at the heart of things here. Have you noticed that Amsterdam's concentric canals resemble the circles of hell? The middle-class hell, of course, peopled with bad dreams. When one comes from the outside, as one gradually goes through those circles, life—and hence its crimes—becomes denser, darker. Here, we are in the last circle. The circle of the ... Ah, you know that? By heaven, you become harder to classify. But you understand then why I can say that the center of things is here, although we stand at the tip of the continent. A sensitive man grasps such oddities. In any case, the newspaper readers and the fornicators can go no further. They come from the four corners of Europe and stop facing the inner sea, on the drab strand. They listen to the foghorns, vainly try to make out the silhouettes of boats in the fog, then turn back over the canals and go home through the rain. Chilled to the bone, they come and ask in all languages for gin at *Mexico City*. There I wait for them.

Till tomorrow, then, *monsieur et cher compatriote*. No, you will easily find your way now: I'll leave you near this bridge. I never cross a bridge at night. It's the result of a vow. Suppose, after all, that someone should jump in the water. One of two things—either you do likewise to fish him out and, in cold weather, you run a great risk! Or you forsake him there and suppressed dives sometimes leave one strangely aching. Good night. What? Those ladies behind those windows? Dream, monsieur, cheap dream, a trip to the Indies! Those persons perfume themselves with spices. You go in, they draw the curtains, and the navigation begins. The gods come down onto the naked bodies and the islands are set adrift, lost souls crowned with the tousled hair of palm trees in the wind. Try it.

II

WHAT is a judge-penitent? Ah, I intrigued you with that business. I meant no harm by it, believe me, and I can explain myself more clearly. In a way, that even belongs to my official duties. But first I must set forth a certain number of facts that will help you to understand my story.

A few years ago I was a lawyer in Paris and, indeed, a rather well-known lawyer. Of course, I didn't tell you my real name. I had a specialty: noble cases. Widows and orphans, as the saying goes—I don't know why, because there are improper widows and ferocious orphans. Yet it was enough for me to sniff the slightest scent of victim on a defendant for me to swing into action. And what action! A real tornado! My heart was on my sleeve. You would really have thought that justice slept with me every night. I am sure you would have admired the rightness of my tone, the appropriateness of my emotion, the persuasion and warmth, the restrained indignation of my speeches before the court. Nature favored me as to my physique, and the noble attitude comes effortlessly. Furthermore, I was buoyed up by two sincere feelings: the satisfaction of being on the right side of the bar and an instinctive scorn for judges in general. That scorn, after all, wasn't perhaps so instinctive. I know now that it had its reasons. But, seen from the outside, it looked rather like a passion. It can't be denied that, for the moment at least, we have to have judges, don't we? However, I could not understand how a man could offer himself to perform such a surprising function. I accepted the fact because I saw it, but rather as I accepted locusts. With this difference: that the invasions of those Orthoptera never brought me a son whereas I earned my living by carrying on a dialogue with people I scorned.

But, after all, I was on the right side; that was enough to satisfy my conscience. The feeling of the law, the satisfaction of being right, the joy of self-esteem, *cher monsieur,* are powerful incentives for keeping us upright or keeping us moving forward. On the other hand, if you deprive men of them, you transform them into dogs frothing with rage. How many crimes committed merely because their authors could not endure being wrong! I once knew a manufacturer who had a perfect wife, admired by all, and yet he deceived her. That man was literally furious to be in the wrong, to be blocked from receiving, or granting himself, a certificate of virtue. The more virtues his wife manifested, the more vexed he became. Eventually, living in the wrong became unbearable to him. What do you think he did then? He gave up deceiving her? Not at all. He killed her. That is how I entered into relations with him.

My situation was more enviable. Not only did I run no risk of joining the criminal camp (in particular I had no chance of killing my wife, being a bachelor), but I even took up their defense, on the sole condition that they should be noble murderers, as others are noble savages. The very manner in which I conducted that defense gave me great satisfactions. I was truly above reproach in my professional life. I never accepted a bribe, it goes without saying, and I never stooped either to any shady proceedings. And—this is even rarer—I never deigned to flatter any journalist to get him on my side, nor any civil servant whose friendship might be useful to me. I even had the luck of seeing the Legion of Honor offered to me two or three times and of being able to refuse it with a discreet dignity in which I found my true reward. Finally, I never charged the poor a fee and never boasted of it. Don't think for a moment, *cher monsieur,* that I am bragging. I take no credit for this. The avidity which in our society substitutes for ambition has always made me laugh. I was aiming higher; you will see that the expression is exact in my case.

But you can already imagine my satisfaction. I enjoyed my own nature to the fullest, and we all know that there lies happiness, although, to soothe one another mutually, we occasionally pretend to condemn such joys as selfishness. At least I enjoyed that part of my nature which reacted so appropriately to the widow and orphan that eventually, through exercise, it came to dominate my whole life. For instance, I loved to help blind people cross streets. From as far away as I could see a cane hesitating on the edge of a sidewalk, I would rush forward, sometimes only a second ahead of another charitable hand already outstretched, snatch the blind person from any solicitude but mine, and lead him gently but firmly along the crosswalk among the traffic obstacles toward the refuge of the other sidewalk, where we would separate with a mutual emotion. In the same way, I always enjoyed giving directions in the street, obliging with a light, lending a hand to heavy pushcarts, pushing a stranded car, buying a paper from the

Salvation Army lass or flowers from the old peddler, though I knew she stole them from the Montparnasse cemetery. I also liked—and this is harder to say—I liked to give alms. A very Christian friend of mine admitted that one's initial feeling on seeing a beggar approach one's house is unpleasant. Well, with me it was worse: I used to exult. But let's not dwell on this.

Let us speak rather of my courtesy. It was famous and unquestionable. Indeed, good manners provided me with great delights. If I had the luck, certain mornings, to give up my seat in the bus or subway to someone who obviously deserved it, to pick up some object an old lady had dropped and return it to her with a smile I knew well, or merely to forfeit my taxi to someone in a greater hurry than I, it was a red-letter day. I even rejoiced, I must admit, those days when the transport system being on strike I had a chance to load into my car at the bus stops some of my unfortunate fellow citizens unable to get home. Giving up my seat in the theater to allow a couple to sit together, hoisting a girl's suitcases onto the rack in a train—these were all deeds I performed more often than others because I paid more attention to the opportunities and was better able to relish the pleasure they give.

Consequently I was considered generous, and so I was. I gave a great deal in public and in private. But far from suffering when I had to give up an object or a sum of money, I derived constant pleasures from this—among them a sort of melancholy which occasionally rose within me at the thought of the sterility of those gifts and the probable ingratitude that would follow. I even took such pleasure in giving that I hated to be obliged to do so. Exactitude in money matters bored me to death and I conformed ungraciously. I had to be the master of my liberalities.

These are just little touches but they will help you grasp the constant delights I experienced in my life, and especially in my profession. Being stopped in the corridor of the law courts by the wife of a defendant you represented out of justice or pity alone—I mean without charge—hearing that woman whisper that nothing, no, nothing could ever repay what you had done for them, replying that it was quite natural, that anyone would have done as much, even offering some financial help to tide over the bad days ahead, then—in order to cut the effusions short and preserve their proper resonance—kissing the hand of a poor woman and breaking away—believe me, *cher monsieur*, this is achieving more than the vulgar ambitious man and rising to that supreme summit where virtue is its own reward.

Let's pause on these heights. Now you understand what I meant when I spoke of aiming higher. I was talking, it so happens, of those supreme summits, the only places I can really live. Yes, I have never felt comfortable except in lofty places. Even in the details of daily life, I needed to feel *above.* I preferred the bus to the subway, open carriages to taxis, terraces to closed-in places. An enthusiast for sport planes in which one's head is in the open, on boats I was the eternal pacer of the top deck. In the mountains I used to flee the deep valleys for the passes and plateaus; I was the man of the mesas at least. If fate had forced me to choose between work at a lathe or as a roofer, don't worry, I'd have chosen the roofs and become acquainted with dizziness. Coalbins, ships' holds, undergrounds, grottoes, pits were repulsive to me. I had even developed a special loathing for speleologists, who had the nerve to fill the front page of our newspapers, and whose records nauseated me. Striving to reach elevation minus eight hundred at the risk of getting one's head caught in a rocky funnel (a siphon, as those fools say!) seemed to me the exploit of perverted or traumatized characters. There was something criminal underlying it.

A natural balcony fifteen hundred feet above a sea still visible bathed in sunlight, on the other hand, was the place where I could breathe most freely, especially if I were alone, well above the human ants. I could readily understand why sermons, decisive preachings, and fire miracles took place on accessible heights. In my opinion no one meditated in cellars or prison cells (unless they were situated in a tower with a broad view); one just became moldy. And I could understand that man who, having entered holy orders, gave up the frock because his cell, instead of overlooking a vast landscape as he expected, looked out on a wall. Rest assured that as far as I was concerned I did not grow moldy. At every hour of the day, within myself and among others, I would scale the heights and light conspicuous fires, and a joyful greeting would rise toward me. Thus at least I took pleasure in life and in my own excellence.

My profession satisfied most happily that vocation for summits. It cleansed me of all bitterness toward my neighbor, whom I always obligated without ever owing him anything. It set me above the judge whom I judged in turn, above the defendant whom I forced to gratitude. Just weigh this, *cher monsieur,* I lived with impunity. I was concerned in no judgment; I was not on the floor of the courtroom, but somewhere in the flies like those gods that are brought down by machinery from time to time to transfigure the action and give it its meaning. After all, living aloft is still the only way of being seen and hailed by the largest number.

Besides, some of my good criminals had killed in obedience to the same feeling. Reading the newspapers afterward, in the sorry condition in which they then were, doubtless brought them a sort of unhappy compensation. Like many men, they had no longer been able to endure anonymity, and that impatience had contributed to leading them to unfortunate extremities. To achieve notoriety it is enough, after all, to kill one's concierge. Unhappily, this is usually an ephemeral reputation, so many concierges are there who deserve and receive the knife. Crime constantly monopolizes the headlines, but the criminal appears there only fugitively, to be replaced at once. In short, such brief triumphs cost too dear. Defending our unfortunate aspirants after a reputation amounted, on the other hand, to becoming really well known, at the same time and in the same places, but by more economical means. Consequently this encouraged me to making more meritorious efforts so that they would pay as little as possible. What they were paying they were doing so to some extent in my place. The indignation, talent, and emotion I expended on them washed away, in return, any debt I might feel toward them. The judges punished and the defendants expiated, while I, free of any duty, shielded from judgment as from penalty, I freely held sway bathed in a light as of Eden.

Indeed, wasn't that Eden, *cher monsieur*: no intermediary between life and me? Such was my life. I never had to learn how to live. In that regard, I already knew everything at birth. Some people's problem is to protect themselves from men or at least to come to terms with them. In my case, the understanding was already established. Familiar when it was appropriate, silent when necessary, capable of a free and easy manner as readily as of dignity, I was always in harmony. Hence my popularity was great and my successes in society innumerable. I was acceptable in appearance; I revealed myself to be both a tireless dancer and an unobtrusively learned man; I managed to love simultaneously—and this is not easy—women and justice; I indulged in sports and the fine arts—in short, I'll not go on for fear you might suspect me of self-flattery. But just imagine, I beg you, a man at the height of his powers, in perfect health, generously gifted, skilled in bodily exercises as in those of the mind, neither rich nor poor, sleeping well, and fundamentally pleased with himself without showing this otherwise than by a felicitous sociability. You will readily see how I can speak, without immodesty, of a successful life.

Yes, few creatures were more natural than I. I was altogether in harmony with life, fitting into it from top to bottom without rejecting any of its ironies, its grandeur, or its servitude. In particular the flesh, matter, the physical in short, which disconcerts or discourages so many men in love or in solitude, without enslaving me, brought me steady joys. I was made to have a body. Whence that harmony in me, that relaxed mastery that people felt, even to telling me sometimes that it helped them in life. Hence my company was in demand. Often, for instance, people thought they had met me before. Life, its creatures and its gifts, offered themselves to me, and I accepted such marks of homage with a kindly pride. To tell the truth, just from being so fully and simply a man, I looked upon myself as something of a superman.

I was of respectable but humble birth (my father was an officer), and yet, certain mornings, let me confess it humbly, I felt like a king's son, or a burning bush. It was not a matter, mind you, of the certainty I had of being more intelligent than everyone else. Besides, such certainty is of no consequence because so many imbeciles share it. No, as a result of being showered with blessings, I felt, I hesitate to admit, marked out. Personally marked out, among all, for that long and uninterrupted success. This, after all, was a result of my modesty. I refused to attribute that success to my own merits and could not believe that the conjunction in a single person of such different and such extreme virtues was the result of chance alone. This is why in my happy life I felt somehow that that happiness was authorized by some higher decree. When I add that I had no religion you can see even better how extraordinary that conviction was. Whether ordinary or not, it served for some time to raise me above the daily routine and I literally soared for a period of years, for which, to tell the truth, I still long in my heart of hearts. I soared until the evening when ... But no, that's another matter and it must be forgotten. Anyway, I am perhaps exaggerating. I was at ease in everything, to be sure, but at the same time satisfied with nothing. Each joy made me desire another. I went from festivity to festivity. On occasion I danced for nights on end, ever madder about people and life. At times, late on those nights when the dancing, the slight intoxication, my wild enthusiasm, everyone's violent unrestraint would fill me with a tired and overwhelmed rapture, it would seem to me—at the breaking point of fatigue and for a second's flash—that at last I understood the secret of creatures and of the world. But my fatigue would disappear the next day, and with it the secret; I would rush forth anew. I ran on like that, always heaped with favors, never satiated, without knowing where to stop, until the day—until the evening rather when the music stopped and the lights went out. The gay party at which I had been so happy ... But allow me to call on our friend the primate. Nod your head to thank him and, above all, drink up with me, I need your understanding.

I see that that declaration amazes you. Have you never suddenly needed understanding, help, friendship? Yes, of course. I have learned to be satisfied with understanding. It is found more readily and, besides, it's not binding. "I beg you to believe in my sympathetic understanding" in the inner discourse always precedes immediately "and now, let's turn to other matters." It's a board chairman's emotion; it comes cheap, after catastrophes. Friendship is less simple. It is long and hard to obtain, but when one has it there's no getting rid of it; one simply has to cope with it. Don't think for a minute that your friends will telephone you every evening, as they ought to, in order to find out if this doesn't happen to be the evening when you are deciding to commit suicide, or simply whether you don't need company, whether you are not in a mood to go out. No, don't worry, they'll ring up the evening you are not alone, when life is beautiful. As for suicide, they would be more likely to push you to it, by virtue of what you owe to yourself, according to them. May heaven protect us, *cher monsieur*, from being set on a pedestal by our friends! Those whose duty is to love us—I mean relatives and connections (what an expression!)—are another matter. They find the right word, all right, and it hits the bull's-eye; they telephone as if shooting a rifle. And they know how to aim. Oh, the Bazaines!

What? What evening? I'll get to it, be patient with me. In a certain way I *am* sticking to my subject with all that about friends and connections. You see, I've heard of a man whose friend had been imprisoned and who slept on the floor of his room every night in order not to enjoy a comfort of which his friend had been deprived. Who, *cher monsieur*, will sleep on the floor for us? Whether I am capable of it myself? Look, I'd like to be and I shall be. Yes, we shall all be capable of it one day, and that will be salvation. But it's not easy, for friendship is absent-minded or at least unavailing. It is incapable of achieving what it wants. Maybe, after all, it doesn't want it enough? Maybe we don't love life enough? Have you noticed that death alone awakens our feelings? How we love the friends who have just left us? How we admire those of our teachers who have ceased to speak, their mouths filled with earth! Then the expression of admiration springs forth naturally, that admiration they were perhaps expecting from us all their lives. But do you know why we are always more just and more generous toward the dead? The reason is simple. With them there is no obligation. They leave us free and we can take our time, fit the testimonial in between a cocktail party and a nice little mistress, in our spare time, in short. If they forced us to anything, it would be to remembering, and we have a short memory. No, it is the recently dead we love among our friends, the painful dead, our emotion, ourselves after all!

For instance, I had a friend I generally avoided. He rather bored me, and, besides, he was something of a moralist. But when he was on his death bed, I was there—don't worry. I never missed a day. He died satisfied with me, holding both my hands. A woman who used to chase after me, and in vain, had the good sense to die young. What room in my heart at once! And when, in addition, it's a suicide! Lord, what a delightful commotion! One's telephone rings, one's heart overflows, and the intentionally short sentences yet heavy with implications, one's restrained suffering and even, yes, a bit of self-accusation!

That's the way man is, *cher monsieur*. He has two faces: he can't love without self-love. Notice your neighbors if perchance a death takes place in the building. They were asleep in their little routine and suddenly, for example, the concierge dies. At once they awake, bestir themselves, get the details, commiserate. A newly dead man and the show begins at last. They need tragedy, don't you know; it's their little transcendence, their *apéritif*. Moreover, is it mere chance that I should speak of a concierge? I had one, really ill favored, malice incarnate, a monster of insignificance and rancor, who would have discouraged a Franciscan. I had even given up speaking to him, but by his mere existence he compromised my customary contentedness. He died and I went to his funeral. Can you tell me why?

Anyway, the two days preceding the ceremony were full of interest. The concierge's wife was ill, lying in the single room, and near her the coffin had been set on sawhorses. Everyone had to get his mail himself. You opened the door, said *"Bonjour, madame,"* listened to her praise of the dear departed as she pointed to him, and took your mail. Nothing very amusing about that. And yet the whole building passed through her room, which stank of carbolic acid. And the tenants didn't send their servants either; they came themselves to take advantage of the unexpected attraction. The servants did too, of course, but on the sly. The day of the funeral, the coffin was too big for the door. "Oh my dearie," the wife said from her bed with a surprise at once delighted and grieved, "how big he was!" "Don't worry, *madame*," replied the funeral director, "we'll get him through edgewise, and upright." He was got through upright and then laid down again, and I was the only one (with a former cabaret doorman who, I gathered, used to drink his Pernod every evening with the doparted) to go as far as the cemetery and strew flowers on a coffin of astounding luxury. Then I paid a visit to the concierge's wife to receive her thanks expressed as by a great tragedienne. Tell me, what was the reason for all that? None, except the *apértif.*

I likewise buried an old fellow member of the Lawyers' Guild. A clerk to whom no one paid attention, but I always shook his hand. Where I worked I used to shake everyone's hand, moreover, being doubly sure to miss no one. Without much effort, such cordial simplicity won me the popularity so necessary to my contentment. For the funeral of our clerk the President of the Guild had not gone out of his way. But I did, and on the eve of a trip, as was amply pointed out. It so happened that I knew my presence would be noticed and favorably commented on. Hence, you see, not even the snow that was falling that day made me withdraw.

What? I'm getting to it, never fear; besides, I have never left it. But let me first point out that my concierge's wife, who had gone to such an out lay for the crucifix, heavy oak, and silver handles in order to get the most out of her emotion, had shacked up a month later with an overdressed yokel proud of his singing voice. He used to beat her; frightful screams could be heard and immediately afterward he would open the window and give forth with his favorite song: "Women, how pretty you are!" "All the *same!*" the neighbors would say. All the same what? I ask you. All right, appearances were against the baritone, and against the concierge's wife, too. But nothing proves that they were not in love. And nothing proves either that she did not love her husband. Moreover, when the yokel took flight, his voice and arm exhausted, she —that faithful wife—resumed her praises of the departed. After all, I know of others who have appearances on their side and are no more faithful or sincere. I knew a man who gave twenty years of his life to a scatterbrained woman, sacrificing everything to her, his friendships, his work, the very respectability of his life, and who one evening recognized that he had never loved her. He had been bored, that's all, bored like most people. Hence he had made himself out of whole cloth a life full of complications and drama. Something must happen—and that explains most human commitments. Something must happen, even loveless slavery, even war or death. Hurray then for funerals!

But I at least didn't have that excuse. I was not bored because I was riding on the crest of the wave. On the evening I am speaking about I can say that I was even less bored than ever. And yet ... You see, *cher monsieur,* it was a fine autumn evening, still warm in town and already damp over the Seine. Night was falling; the sky, still bright in the west, was darkening; the street lamps were glowing dimly. I was walking up the quays of the Left Bank toward the Pont des Arts. The river was gleaming between the stalls of the secondhand booksellers. There were but few people on the quays; Paris was already at dinner. I was treading on the dusty yellow leaves that still recalled summer. Gradually the sky was filling with stars that could be seen for a moment after leaving one street lamp and heading toward another. I enjoyed the return of silence, the evening's mildness, the emptiness of Paris. I was happy. The day had been good: a blind man, the reduced sentence I had hoped for, a cordial handclasp from my client, a few liberalities, and in the afternoon, a brilliant improvisation in the company of several friends on the hardheartedness of our governing class and the hypocrisy of our leaders.

I had gone up on the Pont des Arts, deserted at that hour, to look at the river that could hardly be made out now night had come. Facing the statue of the Vert-Galant, I dominated the island. I felt rising within me a vast feeling of power and—I don't know how to express it—of completion, which cheered my heart. I straightened up and was about to light a cigarette, the cigarette of satisfaction, when, at that very moment, a laugh burst out behind me. Taken by surprise, I suddenly wheeled around; there was no one there. I stepped to the railing; no barge or boat. I turned back toward the island and, again, heard the laughter behind me, a little farther off as if it were going downstream. I stood there motionless. The sound of the laughter was decreasing, but I could still hear it distinctly behind me, come from nowhere unless from the water. At the same time I was aware of the rapid beating of my heart. Please don't misunderstand me; there was nothing mysterious about that laugh; it was a good, hearty, almost friendly laugh, which re-established the proper proportions. Soon I heard nothing more, anyway. I returned to the quays, went up the rue Dauphine, bought some cigarettes I didn't need at all. I was dazed and had trouble breathing. That evening I rang up a friend, who wasn't at home. I was hesitating about going out when, suddenly, I heard laughter under my windows. I opened them. On the sidewalk, in fact, some youths were loudly saying good night. I shrugged my shoulders as I closed the windows; after all, I had a brief to study. I went into the bathroom to drink a glass of water. My reflection was smiling in the mirror, but it seemed to me that my smile was double ...

What? Forgive me, I was thinking of something else. I'll see you again tomorrow, probably. Tomorrow, yes, that's right.

No, no, I can't stay. Besides, I am called in consultation by that brown bear of a man you see over there. A decent fellow, for sure, whom the police are meanly persecuting out of sheer perversity. You think he looks like a killer? Rest assured that his actions conform to his looks. He burgles likewise, and you will be surprised to learn that that cave man is specialized in the art trade. In Holland everyone is a specialist in paintings and in tulips. This one, with his modest mien, is the author of the most famous theft of a painting. Which one? I may tell you. Don't be surprised at my knowledge. Although I am a judge-penitent, I have my side line here: I am the legal counselor of these good people. I studied the laws of the country and built up a clientele in this quarter where diplomas are not required. It wasn't easy, but I inspire confidence, don't I? I have a good, hearty laugh and an energetic handshake, and those are trump cards. Besides, I settled a few difficult cases, out of self-interest to begin with and later out of conviction. If pimps and thieves were invariably sentenced, all decent people would get to thinking they themselves were constantly innocent, *cher monsieur*. And in my opinion—all right, all right, I'm coming!—that's what must be avoided above all. Otherwise, everything would be just a joke.

III

Really, *mon cher compatriote*, I am grateful to you for your curiosity. However, there is nothing extraordinary about my story. Since you are interested, I'll tell you that I thought a little about that laugh, for a few days, then forgot about it. Once in a great while, I seemed to hear it within me. But most of the time, without making any effort, I thought of other things.

Yet I must admit that I ceased to walk along the Paris quays. When I would ride along them in a car or bus, a sort of silence would descend on me. I was waiting, I believe. But I would cross the Seine, nothing would happen, and I would breathe again. I also had some health problems at that time. Nothing definite, a dejection perhaps, a sort of difficulty in recovering my good spirits. I saw doctors, who gave me stimulants. I was alternately stimulated and depressed. Life became less easy for me: when the body is sad the heart languishes. It seemed to me that I was half unlearning what I had never learned and yet knew so well—how to live. Yes, I think it was probably then that everything began.

But this evening I don't feel quite up to snuff either. I even find trouble expressing myself. I'm not talking so well, it seems to me, and my words are less assured. Probably the weather. It's hard to breathe; the air is so heavy it weighs on one's chest. Would you object, *mon cher compatriote*, to going out and walking in the town a little? Thank you.

How beautiful the canals are this evening! I like the breath of stagnant waters, the smell of dead leaves soaking in the canal and the funereal scent rising from the barges loaded with flowers. No, no, there's nothing morbid about such a taste, I assure you. On the contrary, it's deliberate with me. The truth is that I force myself to admire these canals. What I like most in the world is Sicily, you see, and especially from the top of Etna, in the sunlight, provided I dominate the island and the sea. Java, too, but at the time of the trade winds. Yes, I went there in my youth. In a general way, I like all islands. It is easier to dominate them.

Charming house, isn't it? The two heads you see up there are heads of Negro slaves. A shop sign. The house belonged to a slave dealer. Oh, they weren't squeamish in those days! They had assurance; they announced: "You see, I'm a man of substance; I'm in the slave trade; I deal in black flesh." Can you imagine anyone today making it known publicly that such is his business? What a scandal! I can hear my Parisian colleagues right now. They are adamant on the subject; they wouldn't hesitate to launch two or three manifestoes, maybe even more! And on reflection, I'd add my signature to theirs. Slavery?—certainly not, we are against it! That we should be forced to establish it at home or in our factories—well, that's natural; but boasting about it, that's the limit!

I am well aware that one can't get along without domineering or being served. Every man needs slaves as he needs fresh air. Commanding is breathing—you agree with me? And even the most destitute manage to breathe. The lowest man in the social scale still has his wife or his child. If he's unmarried, a dog. The essential thing, after all, is being able to get angry with someone who has no right to talk back. "One doesn't talk back to one's father"—you know the expression? In one way it is very odd. To whom should one talk back in this world if not to what one loves? In another way, it is convincing. Somebody has to have the last word. Otherwise, every reason can be answered with another one and there would never be an end to it. Power, on the other hand, settles everything. It took time, but we finally realized that. For instance, you must have noticed that our old Europe at last philosophizes in the right way. We no longer say as in simple times: "This is the way I think. What are your objections?" We have become lucid. For the dialogue we have substituted the communiqué: "This is the truth," we say. "You can discuss it as much as you want; we aren't interested. But in a few years there'll be the police who will show you we are right."

Ah, this dear old planet! All is clear now. We know ourselves; we now know of what we are capable. Just take me, to change examples if not subjects, I have always wanted to be served with a smile. If the maid looked sad, she poisoned my days. She had a right not to be cheerful, to be sure. But I told myself that it was better for her to perform her service with a laugh than with tears. In fact, it was better for me. Yet, without boasting, my reasoning was not altogether idiotic. Likewise, I always refused to eat in Chinese restaurants. Why? Because Orientals when they are silent and in the presence of whites often look scornful. Naturally they keep that look when serving. How then can you enjoy the glazed chicken? And, above all, how can you look at them and think you are right?

Just between us, slavery, preferably with a smile, is inevitable then. But we must not admit it. Isn't it better that whoever cannot do without having slaves should call them free men? For the principle to begin with, and, secondly, not to drive them to despair. We owe them that compensation, don't we? In that way, they will continue to smile and we shall maintain our good conscience. Otherwise, we'd be obliged to reconsider our opinion of ourselves; we'd go mad with suffering, or even become modest—for everything would be possible. Consequently, no shop signs, and this one is shocking. Besides, if everyone told all, displayed his true profession and identity, we shouldn't know which way to turn! Imagine the visiting cards: Dupont, jittery philosopher, or Christian landowner, or adulterous humanist—indeed, there's a wide choice. But it would be hell! Yes, hell must be like that: streets filled with shop signs and no way of explaining oneself. One is classified once and for all.

You, for instance, *mon cher compatriote*, stop and think of what your sign would be. You are silent? Well, you'll tell me later on. I know mine in any case: a double face, a charming Janus, and above it the motto of the house: "Don't rely on it." On my cards: "Jean-Baptiste Clamence, play actor." Why, shortly after the evening I told you about, I discovered something. When I would leave a blind man on the sidewalk to which I had convoyed him, I used to tip my hat to him. Obviously the hat tipping wasn't intended for him, since he couldn't see it. To whom was it addressed? To the public. After playing my part, I would take the bow. Not bad, eh? Another day during the same period, to a motorist who was thanking me for helping him, I replied that no one would have done as much. I meant, of course, anyone. But that unfortunate slip weighed heavy on me. For modesty, really, I took the cake.

I have to admit it humbly, *mon cher compatriote*, I was always bursting with vanity. I, I, I is the refrain of my whole life, which could be heard in everything I said. I could never talk without boasting, especially if I did so with that shattering discretion that was my specialty. It is quite true that I always lived free and powerful. I simply felt released in regard to all for the excellent reason that I recognized no equals. I always considered myself more intelligent than everyone else, as I've told you, but also more sensitive and more skillful, a crack shot, an incomparable driver, a better lover. Even in the fields in which it was easy for me to verify my inferiority—like tennis, for instance, in which I was but a passable partner—it was hard for me not to think that, with a little time for practice, I would surpass the best players. I admitted only superiorities in me and this explained my good will and serenity. When I was concerned with others, I was so out of pure condescension, in utter freedom, and all the credit went to me: my self-esteem would go up a degree.

Along with a few other truths, I discovered these facts little by little in the period following the evening I told you about. Not all at once nor very clearly. First I had to recover my memory. By gradual degress I saw more clearly, I learned a little of what I knew. Until then I had always been aided by an extraordinary ability to forget. I used to forget everything, beginning with my resolutions. Fundamentally, nothing mattered. War, suicide, love, poverty got my attention, of course, when circumstances forced me, but a courteous, superficial attention. At times, I would pretend to get excited about some cause foreign to my daily life. But basically I didn't really take part in it except, of course, when my freedom was thwarted. How can I express it? Everything slid off— yes, just rolled off me.

In the interest of fairness, it should be said that sometimes my forgetfulness was praiseworthy. You have noticed that there are people whose religion consists in forgiving all offenses, and who do in fact forgive them but never forget them? I wasn't good enough to forgive offenses, but eventually I always forgot them. And the man who thought I hated him couldn't get over seeing me tip my hat to him with a smile. According to his nature, he would then admire my nobility of character or scorn my ill breeding without realizing that my reason was simpler: I had forgotten his very name. The same infirmity that often made me indifferent or ungrateful in such cases made me magnanimous.

I lived consequently without any other continuity than that, from day to day, of I, I, I. From day to day women, from day to day virtue or vice, from day to day, like dogs—but every day myself secure at my post. Thus I progressed on the surface of life, in the realm of words as it were, never in reality. All those books barely read, those friends barely loved, those cities barely visited, those women barely possessed! I went through the gestures out of boredom or absentmindedness. Then came human beings; they wanted to cling, but there was nothing to cling to, and that was unfortunate—for them. As for me, I forgot. I never remembered anything but myself.

Gradually, however, my memory returned. Or rather, I returned to it, and in it I found the recollection that was awaiting me. But before telling you of it, allow me, *mon cher compatriote*, to give you a few examples (they will be useful to you, I am sure) of what I discovered in the course of my exploration.

One day in my car when I was slow in making a getaway at the green light while our patient fellow citizens immediately began honking furiously behind me, I suddenly remembered another occasion set in similar circumstances. A motorcycle ridden by a spare little man wearing spectacles and plus fours had gone around me and planted itself in front of me at the red light. As he came to a stop the little man had stalled his motor and was vainly striving to revive it. When the light changed, I asked him with my usual courtesy to take his motorcycle out of my way so I might pass. The little man was getting irritable over his wheezy motor. Hence he replied, according to the rules of Parisian courtesy, that I could go climb a tree. I insisted, still polite, but with a slight shade of impatience in my voice. I was immediately told that in any case I could go straight to hell. Meanwhile several horns began to be heard behind me. With greater firmness I begged my interlocutor to be polite and to realize that he was blocking traffic. The irascible character, probably exasperated by the now evident ill will of his motor, informed me that if I wanted what he called a thorough dusting off he would gladly give it to me. Such cynicism filled me with a healthy rage and I got out of my car with the intention of thrashing this coarse individual. I don't think I am cowardly (but what doesn't one think!); I was a head taller than my adversary and my muscles have always been reliable. I still believe the dusting off would have been received rather than given. But I had hardly set foot on the pavement when from the gathering crowd a man stepped forth, rushed at me, assured me that I was the lowest of the low and that he would not allow me to strike a man who had a motorcycle between his legs and hence was at a disadvantage. I turned toward this musketeer and, in truth, didn't even see him. Indeed, hardly had I turned my head when, almost simultaneously, I heard the motorcycle begin popping again and received a violent blow on the ear. Before I had the time to register what had happened, the motorcycle rode away. Dazed, I mechanically walked toward d'Artagnan when, at the same moment, an exasperated concert of horns rose from the now considerable line of vehicles. The light was changing to green. Then, still somewhat bewildered, instead of giving a drubbing to the idiot who had addressed me, I docilely returned to my car and drove off. As I passed, the idiot greeted me with a "poor dope" that I still recall.

A totally insignificant story, in your opinion? Probably. Still it took me some time to forget it, and that's what counts. Yet I had excuses. I had let myself be beaten without replying, but I could not be accused of cowardice. Taken by surprise, addressed from both sides, I had mixed everything up and the horns had put the finishing touch to my embarrassment. Yet I was unhappy about this as if I had violated the code of honor. I could see myself getting back into my car without a reaction, under the ironic gaze of a crowd especially delighted because, as I recall, I was wearing a very elegant blue suit. I could hear the "poor dope" which, in spite of everything, struck me as justified. In short, I had collapsed in public. As a result of a series of circumstances, to be sure, but there are always circumstances. As an afterthought I clearly saw what I should have done. I saw myself felling d'Artagnan with a good hook to the jaw, getting back into my car, pursuing the monkey who had struck me, overtaking him, jamming his machine against the curb, taking him aside, and giving him the licking he had fully deserved. With a few variants, I ran off this little film a hundred times in my imagination. But it was too late, and for several days I chewed a bitter resentment.

Why, it's raining again. Let's stop, shall we, under this portico? Good. Where was I? Oh, yes, honor! Well, when I recovered the recollection of that episode, I realized what it meant. After all, my dream had not stood up to facts. I had dreamed—this was now clear—of being a complete man who managed to make himself respected in his person as well as in his profession. Half Cerdan, half de Gaulle, if you will. In short, I wanted to dominate in all things. This is why I assumed the man- ner, made a particular point of displaying my physical skill rather than my intellectual gifts. But after having been struck in public without reacting, it was no longer possible for me to cherish that fine picture of myself. If I had been the friend of truth and intelligence I claimed to be, what would that episode have mattered to me? It was already forgotten by those who had witnessed it. I'd have barely accused myself of having got angry over nothing and also, having got angry, of not having managed to face up to the consequences of my anger, for want of presence of mind. Instead of that, I was eager to get my revenge, to strike and conquer. As if my true desire were not to be the most intelligent or most generous creature on earth, but only to beat anyone I wanted, to be the stronger, in short, and in the most elementary way. The truth is that every intelligent man, as you know, dreams of being a gangster and of ruling over society by force alone. As it is not so easy as the detective novels might lead one to believe, one generally relies on politics and joins the cruelest party. What does it matter, after all, if by humiliating one's mind one succeeds in dominating everyone? I discovered in myself sweet dreams of oppression.

I learned at least that I was on the side of the guilty, the accused, only in exactly so far as their crime caused me no harm. Their guilt made me eloquent because I was not its victim. When I was threatened, I became not only a judge in turn but even more: an irascible master who wanted, regardless of all laws, to strike down the offender and get him on his knees. After that, *mon cher compatriote*, it is very hard to continue seriously believing one has a vocation for justice and is the predestined defender of the widow and orphan.

Since the rain is coming down harder and we have the time, may I impart to you another dis- covery I made, soon after, in my memory? Let's sit down on this bench out of the rain. For cen- turies pipe smokers have been watching the same rain falling on the same canal. What I have to tell you is a bit more difficult. This time it concerns a woman. To begin with, you must know that I always succeeded with women—and without much effort. I don't say succeed in making them happy or even in making myself happy through them. No, simply succeed. I used to achieve my ends just about whenever I wanted I was considered to have charm. Fancy that! You know what charm is: a way of getting the answer yes without having asked any clear question. And that was true of me at the time. Does that surprise you? Come now, don't deny it. With the face I now have, that's quite natural. Alas, after a certain age every man is responsible for his face. Mine ... But what matter? It's a fact—I was considered to have charm and I took advantage of it.

Without calculation, however; I was in good faith, or almost. My relationship with women was natural, free, easy, as the saying goes. No guile in it except that obvious guile which they look upon as a homage. I loved them, according to the hallowed expression, which amounts to saying that I never loved any of them. I always considered misogyny vulgar and stupid, and almost all the women I have known seemed to me better than I. Nevertheless, setting them so high, I made use of them more often than I served them. How can one make it out?

Of course, true love is exceptional—two or three times a century, more or less. The rest of the time there is vanity or boredom. As for me, in any case I was not the Portuguese Nun. I am not hard-hearted; far from it—full of pity on the contrary and with a ready tear to boot. Only, my emotional impulses always turn toward me, my feelings of pity concern me. It is not true, after all, that I never loved. I conceived at least one great love in my life, of which I was always the object. From that point of view, after the inevitable hardships of youth, I was early focused: sensuality alone dominated my love life. I looked merely for objects of pleasure and conquest. Moreover, I was aided in this by my constitution: nature had been generous with me. I was considerably proud of this and derived many satisfactions therefrom—without my knowing now whether they were physical or based on prestige. Of course you will say that I am boasting again. I shan't deny it and I am hardly proud of doing so, for here I am boasting of what is true.

In any case, my sensuality (to limit myself to it) was so real that even for a ten-minute adventure I'd have disowned father and mother, even were I to regret it bitterly. Indeed—*especially* for a ten- minute adventure and even more so if I were sure it was to have no sequel. I had principles, to be sure, such as that the wife of a friend is sacred. But I simply ceased quite sincerely, a few days before, to feel any friendship for the husband. Maybe I ought not to call this sensuality? Sensuality is not repulsive. Let's be indulgent and use the word "infirmity," a sort of congenital inability to see in love anything but the physical. That infirmity, after all, was convenient. Combined with my faculty for forgetting, it favored my freedom. At the same time, through a certain appearance of inaccessibility and unshakable independence it gave me, it provided the opportunity for new successes. As a result of not being romantic, I gave romance something to work on. Our feminine friends have in common with Bonaparte the belief that they can succeed where everyone else has failed.

In this exchange, moreover, I satisfied something in addition to my sensuality: my passion for gambling. I loved in women my partners in a certain game, which had at least the taste of innocence. You see, I can't endure being bored and appreciate only diversions in life. Any society, however bril- liant, soon crushes me, whereas I have never been bored with the women I liked. It hurts me to con- fess it, but I'd have given ten conversations with Einstein for an initial rendezvous with a pretty chorus girl. It's true that at the tenth rendezvous I was longing for Einstein or a serious book. In short, I was never concerned with the major problems except in the intervals between my little excesses. And how often, standing on the sidewalk involved in a passionate discussion with friends, I lost the thread of the argument being developed because a devastating woman was crossing the street at that very moment.

Hence I played the game. I knew they didn't like one to reveal one's purpose too quickly. First, there had to be conversation, fond attentions, as they say. I wasn't worried about speeches, being a lawyer, nor about glances, having been an amateur actor during my military service. I often changed parts, but it was always the same play. For instance, the scene of the incomprehensible attraction, of the "mysterious something," of the "it's unreasonable, I certainly didn't want to be attracted, I was even tired of love, etc. ..." always worked, though it is one of the oldest in the repertory. There was also the gambit of the mysterious happiness no other woman has ever given you; it may be a blind alley—indeed, it surely is (for one cannot protect oneself too much)—but it just happens to be unique. Above all, I had perfected a little speech which was always well received and which, I am sure, you will applaud. The essential part of that act lay in the assertion, painful and resigned, that I was nothing, that it was not worth getting involved with me, that my life was elsewhere and not related to everyday happiness—a happiness that maybe I should have preferred to anything, but there you were, it was too late. As to the reasons behind this decisive lateness, I maintained secrecy, knowing that it is always better to go to bed with a mystery. In a way, moreover, I believed what I said; I was living my part. It is not surprising that my partners likewise began to "tread the boards" enthusiastically. The most sensitive among them tried to understand me, and that effort led them to melancholy surrenders. The others, satisfied to note that I was respecting the rules of the game and had the tactfulness to talk before acting, progressed without delay to the realities. This meant I had won—and twice over, since, besides the desire I felt for them, I was satisfying the love I bore myself by verifying each time my special powers.

This is so true that even if some among them provided but slight pleasure, I nevertheless tried to resume relations with them, at long intervals, helped doubtless by that strange desire kindled by absence and a suddenly recovered complicity, but also to verify the fact that our ties still held and that it was my privilege alone to tighten them. Sometimes I went so far as to make them swear not to give themselves to any other man, in order to quiet my worries once and for all on that score. My heart, however, played no part in that worry, nor even my imagination. A certain type of pretension was in fact so personified in me that it was hard for me to imagine, despite the facts, that a woman who had once been mine could ever belong to another. But the oath they swore to me liberated me while it bound them. As soon as I knew they would never belong to anyone, I could make up my mind to break off—which otherwise was almost always impossible for me. As far as they were concerned, I had proved my point once and for all and assured my power for a long time. Strange, isn't it? But that's the way it was, *mon cher compatriote.* Some cry: "Love me!" Others: "Don't love me!" But a certain genus, the worst and most unhappy, cries: "Don't love me and be faithful to me!"

Except that the proof is never definitive, after all; one has to begin again with each new person. As a result of beginning over and over again, one gets in the habit. Soon the speech comes without thinking and the reflex follows; and one day you find yourself taking without really desiring. Believe me, for certain men at least, not taking what one doesn't desire is the hardest thing in the world.

This is what happened eventually and there's no point in telling you who she was except that, without really stirring me, she had attracted me by her passive, avid manner. Frankly, it was a shabby experience, as I should have expected. But I never had any complexes and soon forgot the person, whom I didn't see again. I thought she hadn't noticed anything and didn't even imagine she could have an opinion. Besides, in my eyes her passive manner cut her off from the world. A few weeks later, however, I learned that she had related my deficiencies to a third person. At once I felt as if I had been somewhat deceived; she wasn't so passive as I had thought and she didn't lack judgment. Then I shrugged my shoulders and pretended to laugh. I even laughed outright; clearly the incident was unimportant. If there is any realm in which modesty ought to be the rule, isn't it sex with all the unforeseeable there is in it? But no, each of us tries to show up to advantage, even in solitude. Despite having shrugged my shoulders, what was my behavior in fact? I saw that woman again a little later and did everything necessary to charm her and really take her back. It was not very difficult, for *they* don't like either to end on a failure. From that moment onward, without really intending it, I began, in fact, to mortify her in every way. I would give her up and take her back, force her to give herself at inappropriate times and in inappropriate places, treat her so brutally, in every regard, that eventually I attached myself to her as I imagine the jailer is bound to his prisoner. And this kept up till the day when, in the violent disorder of painful and constrained pleasure, she paid a tribute aloud to what was enslaving her. That very day I began to move away from her. I have forgotten her since.

I'll agree with you, despite your polite silence, that that adventure is not very pretty. But just think of your life, *mon cher compatriote!* Search your memory and perhaps you will find some similar story that you'll tell me later on. In my case, when that business came to mind, I again began to laugh. But it was another kind of laugh, rather like the one I had heard on the Pont des Arts. I was laughing at my speeches and my pleadings in court. Even more at my court pleading than at my speeches to women. To them, at least, I did not lie much. Instinct spoke clearly, without subterfuges, in my attitude. The act of love, for instance, is a confession. Selfishness screams aloud, vanity shows off, or else true generosity reveals itself. Ultimately in that regrettable story, even more than in my other affairs, I had been more outspoken than I thought; I had declared who I was and how I could live. Despite appearances, I was therefore more worthy in my private life—even when (one might say: especially when) I behaved as I have told you—than in my great professional flights about innocence and justice. At least, seeing myself act with others, I couldn't deceive myself as to the truth of my nature. No man is a hypocrite in his pleasures—have I read that or did I think it myself, *mon cher compatriote*?

When I examined thus the trouble I had in separating definitively from a woman—a trouble which used to involve me in so many simultaneous liaisons—I didn't blame my soft-heartedness. That was not what impelled me when one of my mistresses tired of waiting for the Austerlitz of our passion and spoke of leaving me. At once I was the one who made a step forward, who yielded, who became eloquent. As for affection and soft-heartedness, I aroused them in women, experiencing merely the appearance of them myself—simply a little excited by this refusal, alarmed also by the possible loss of someone's affection. At times I truly thought I was suffering, to be sure. But the rebellious female had merely to leave in fact for me to forget her without effort, as I forgot her presence when, on the contrary, she had decided to return. No, it was not love or generosity that awakened me when I was in danger of being forsaken, but merely the desire to be loved and to receive what in my opinion was due me. The moment I was loved and my partner again forgotten, I shone, I was at the top of my form, I became likable.

Be it said, moreover, that as soon as I had re-won that affection I became aware of its weight. In my moments of irritation I told myself that the ideal solution would have been the death of the person I was interested in. Her death would, on the one hand, have definitively fixed our relationship and, on the other, removed its compulsion. But one cannot long for the death of everyone or, in the extreme, depopulate the planet in order to enjoy a freedom that cannot be imagined otherwise. My sensibility was opposed to this, and my love of mankind.

The only deep emotion I occasionally felt in these affairs was gratitude, when all was going well and I was left, not only peace, but freedom to come and go—never kinder and gayer with one woman than when I had just left another's bed, as if I extended to all others the debt I had just contracted toward one of them. In any case, however apparently confused my feelings were, the result I achieved was clear: I kept all my affections within reach to make use of them when I wanted. On my own admission, I could live happily only on condition that all the individuals on earth, or the greatest possible number, were turned toward me, eternally in suspense, devoid of independent life and ready to answer my call at any moment, doomed in short to sterility until the day I should deign to favor them. In short, for me to live happily it was essential for the creatures I chose not to live at all. They must receive their life, sporadically, only at my bidding.

Oh, I don't feel any self-satisfaction, believe me, in telling you this. Upon thinking of that time when I used to ask for everything without paying anything myself, when I used to mobilize so many people in my service, when I used to put them in the refrigerator, so to speak, in order to have them at hand some day when it would suit me, I don't know how to name the odd feeling that comes over me. Isn't it shame, perhaps? Tell me, *mon cher compatriote*, doesn't shame sting a little? It does? Well, it's probably shame, then, or one of those silly emotions that have to do with honor. It seems to me in any case that that feeling has never left me since the adventure I found at the heart of my memory, which I cannot any longer put off relating, despite my digressions and the inventive efforts for which, I hope, you give me credit.

Look, the rain has stopped! Be kind enough to walk home with me. I am strangely tired, not from having talked so much but at the mere thought of what I still have to say. Oh, well, a few words will suffice to relate my essential discovery. What's the use of saying more, anyway? For the statue to stand bare, the fine speeches must take flight like pigeons. So here goes. That particular night in November, two or three years before the evening when I thought I heard laughter behind me, I was returning to the Left Bank and my home by way of the Pont Royal. It was an hour past midnight, a fine rain was falling, a drizzle rather, that scattered the few people on the streets. I had just left a mistress, who was surely already asleep. I was enjoying that walk, a little numbed, my body calmed and irrigated by a flow of blood gentle as the falling rain. On the bridge I passed behind a figure leaning over the railing and seeming to stare at the river. On closer view, I made out a slim young woman dressed in black. The back of her neck, cool and damp between her dark hair and coat collar, stirred me. But I went on after a moment's hesitation. At the end of the bridge I followed the guys toward Saint-Michel, where I lived. I had already gone some fifty yards when I heard the sound—which, despite the distance, seemed dreadfully loud in the midnight silence—of a body striking the water. I stopped short, but without turning around. Almost at once I heard a cry, repeated several times, which was going downstream; then it suddenly ceased. The silence that followed, as the night suddenly stood still, seemed interminable. I wanted to run and yet didn't stir. I was trembling, I believe from cold and shock. I told myself that I had to be quick and I felt an irresistible weakness steal over me. I have forgotten what I thought then. "Too late, too far ..." or something of the sort. I was still listening as I stood motionless. Then, slowly under the rain, I went away. I informed no one.

But here we are; here's my house, my shelter! Tomorrow? Yes, if you wish. I'd like to take you to the island of Marken so you can see the Zuider Zee. Let's meet at eleven at *Mexico City*. What? That woman? Oh, I don't know. Really I don't know. The next day, and the days following, I didn't read the papers.

IV

A DOLL'S village, isn't it? No shortage of quaintness here! But I didn't bring you to this island for quaintness, *cher ami*. Anyone can show you peasant headdresses, wooden shoes, and ornamented houses with fishermen smoking choice tobacco surrounded by the smell of furniture wax. I am one of the few people, on the other hand, who can show you what really matters here.

We are reaching the dike. We'll have to follow it to get as far as possible from these too charming houses. Please, let's sit down. Well, what do you think of it? Isn't it the most beautiful negative landscape? Just see on the left that pile of ashes they call a dune here, the gray dike on the right, the livid beach at our feet, and in front of us, the sea the color of a weak lye-solution with the vast sky reflecting the colorless waters. A soggy hell, indeed! Everything horizontal, no relief; space is colorless, and life dead. Is it not universal obliteration, everlasting nothingness made visible? No hu- man beings, above all, no human beings! You and I alone facing the planet at last deserted! The sky is alive? You are right, *cher ami*. It thickens, becomes concave, opens up air shafts and doses cloudy doors. Those are the doves. Haven't you noticed that the sky of Holland is filled with millions of doves, invisible because of their altitude, which flap their wings, rise or fall in unison, filling the heavenly space with dense multitudes of grayish feathers carried hither and thither by the wind? The doves wait up there all year round. They wheel above the earth, look down, and would like to come down. But there is nothing but the sea and the canals, roofs covered with shop signs, and never a head on which to light.

You don't understand what I mean? I'll admit my fatigue. I lose the thread of what I am saying; I've lost that lucidity to which my friends used to enjoy paying respects. I say "my friends," moreover, as a convention. I have no more friends; I have nothing but accomplices. To make up for this, their number has increased; they are the whole human race. And within the human race, you first of all. Whoever is at hand is always the first. How do I know I have no friends? It's very easy: I discovered it the day I thought of killing myself to play a trick on them, to punish them, in a way. But punish whom? Some would be surprised, and no one would feel punished. I realized I had no friends. Besides, even if I had had, I shouldn't be any better off. If I had been able to commit suicide and then see their reaction, why, then the game would have been worth the candle. But the earth is dark, *cher ami*, the coffin thick, and the shroud opaque, The eyes of the soul—to be sure—if there is a soul and it has eyes! But you see, we're not sure, we can't be sure. Otherwise, there would be a solution; at least one could get oneself taken seriously. Men are never convinced of your reasons, of your sincerity, of the seriousness of your sufferings, except by your death. So long as you are alive, your case is doubtful; you have a right only to their skepticism. So if there were the least certainty that one could enjoy the show, it would be worth proving to them what they are unwilling to believe and thus amazing them. But you kill yourself and what does it matter whether or not they believe you? You are not there to see their amazement and their contrition (fleeting at best), to witness, according to every man's dream, your own funeral. In order to cease being a doubtful case, one has to cease being, that's all.

Besides, isn't it better thus? We'd suffer too much from their indifference. "You'll pay for this!" a daughter said to her father who had prevented her from marrying a too well groomed suitor. And she killed herself. But the father paid for nothing. He loved fly-casting. Three Sundays later he went back to the river—to forget, as he said. He was right; he forgot. To tell the truth, the contrary would have been surprising. You think you are dying to punish your wife and actually you are freeing her. It's better not to see that. Besides the fact that you might hear the reasons they give for your action. As far as I am concerned, I can hear them now: "He killed himself because he couldn't bear ..." Ah, *cher ami*, how poor in invention men are! They always think one commits suicide for a reason. But it's quite possible to commit suicide for two reasons. No, that never occurs to them. So what's the good of dying intentionally, of sacrificing yourself to the idea you want people to have of you? Once you are dead, they will take advantage of it to attribute idiotic or vulgar motives to your action. Martyrs, *cher ami*, must choose between being forgotten, mocked, or made use of. As for being understood—never!

Besides, let's not beat about the bush; I love life—that's my real weakness. I love it so much that I am incapable of imagining what is not life. Such avidity has something plebeian about it, don't you think? Aristocracy cannot imagine itself without a little distance surrounding itself and its life. One dies if necessary, one breaks rather than bending. But I bend, because I continue to love myself. For example, after all I have told you, what do you think I developed? An aversion for myself? Come, come, it was especially with others that I was fed up. To be sure, I knew my failings and regretted them. Yet I continued to forget them with a rather meritorious obstinacy. The prosecution of others, on the contrary, went on constantly in my heart. Of course—does that shock you? Maybe you think it's not logical? But the question is not to remain logical. The question is to slip through and, above all—yes, above all, the question is to elude judgment. I'm not saying to avoid punishment, for punishment without judgment is bearable. It has a name, besides, that guarantees our innocence: it is called misfortune. No, on the contrary, it's a matter of dodging judgment, of avoiding being forever judged without ever having a sentence pronounced.

But one can't dodge it so easily. Today we are always ready to judge as we are to fornicate. With this difference, that there are no inadequacies to fear. If you doubt this, just listen to the table conversation during August in those summer hotels where our charitable fellow citizens take the boredom cure. If you still hesitate to conclude, read the writings of our great men of the moment. Or else observe your own family and you will be edified. *Mon cher ami*, let's not give them any pretext, no matter how small, for judging us! Otherwise, we'll be left in shreds. We are forced to take the same precautions as the animal tamer. If, before going into the cage, he has the misfortune to cut himself while shaving, what a feast for the wild animals! I realized this all at once the moment I had the suspicion that maybe I wasn't so admirable. From then on, I became distrustful. Since I was bleeding slightly, there was no escape for me; they would devour me.

My relations with my contemporaries were apparently the same and yet subtly out of tune. My friends hadn't changed. On occasion, they still extolled the harmony and security they found in my company. But I was aware only of the dissonances and disorder that filled me; I felt vulnerable and open to public accusation. In my eyes my fellows ceased to be the respectful public to which I was accustomed. The circle of which I was the center broke and they lined up in a row as on the judge's bench. In short, the moment I grasped that there was something to judge in me, I realized that there was in them an irresistible vocation for judgment. Yes, they were there as before, but they were laughing. Or rather it seemed to me that every one I encountered was looking at me with a hidden smile. I even had the impression, at that time, that people were tripping me up. Two or three times, in fact, I stumbled as I entered public places. Once, even, I went sprawling on the floor. The Cartesian Frenchman in me didn't take long to catch hold of himself and attribute those accidents to the only reasonable divinity—that is, chance. Nonetheless, my distrust remained.

Once my attention was aroused, it was not hard for me to discover that I had enemies. In my profession, to begin with, and also in my social life. Some among them I had obliged. Others I should have obliged. All that, after all, was natural, and I discovered it without too much grief. It was harder and more painful, on the other hand, to admit that I had enemies among people I hardly knew or didn't know at all. I had always thought, with the ingenuousness I have already illustrated to you, that those who didn't know me couldn't resist liking me if they came to know me. Not at all! I encountered hostility especially among those who knew me only at a distance without my knowing them myself. Doubtless they suspected me of living fully, given up completely to happiness; and that cannot be forgiven. The look of success, when it is worn in a certain way, would infuriate a jackass. Then again, my life was full to bursting, and for lack of time, I used to refuse many advances. Then I would forget my refusals, for the same reason. But those advances had been made me by people whose lives were not full and who, for that very reason, would remember my refusals.

Thus it is that in the end, to take but one example, women cost me dear. The time I used to devote to them I couldn't give to men, who didn't always forgive me this. Is there any way out? Your successes and happiness are forgiven you only if you generously consent to share them. But to be happy it is essential not to be too concerned with others. Consequently, there is no escape. Happy and judged, or absolved and wretched. As for me, the injustice was even greater: I was condemned for past successes. For a long time I had lived in the illusion of a general agreement, whereas, from all sides, judgments, arrows, mockeries rained upon me, inattentive and smiling. The day I was alerted I became lucid; I received all the wounds at the same time and lost my strength all at once. The whole universe then began to laugh at me.

That is what no man (except those who are not really alive—in other words, wise men) can endure. Spitefulness is the only possible ostentation. People hasten to judge in order not to be judged themselves. What do you expect? The idea that comes most naturally to man, as if from his very nature, is the idea of his innocence. From this point of view, we are all like that little Frenchman at Buchenwald who insisted on registering a complaint with the clerk, himself a prisoner, who was recording his arrival. A complaint? The clerk and his comrades laughed: "Useless, old man.

You don't lodge a complaint here." "But you see, sir," said the little Frenchman, "my case is exceptional I am innocent!" We are all exceptional cases. We all want to appeal against something! Each of us insists on being innocent at all cost, even if he has to accuse the whole human race and heaven itself. You won't delight a man by complimenting him on the efforts by which he has become intelligent or generous.

On the other hand, he will beam if you admire his natural generosity. Inversely, if you tell a criminal that his crime is not due to his nature or his character but to unfortunate circumstances, he will be extravagantly grateful to you. During the counsel's speech, this is the moment he will choose to weep. Yet there is no credit in being honest or intelligent by birth. Just as one is surely no more responsible for being a criminal by nature than for being a criminal by circumstance. But those rascals want grace, that is, irresponsibility, and they shamelessly allege the justifications of nature or the excuses of circumstances, even if they are contradictory. The essential thing is that they should be innocent, that their virtues, by grace of birth, should not be questioned and that their misdeeds, born of a momentary misfortune, should never be more than provisional. As I told you, it's a matter of dodging judgment. Since it is hard to dodge it, tricky to get one's nature simultaneously admired and excused, they all strive to be rich. Why? Did you ever ask yourself? For power, of course. But especially because wealth shields from immediate judgment, takes you out of the subway crowd to enclose you in a chromium-plated automobile, isolates you in huge protected lawns, Pullmans, first- class cabins. Wealth, *cher ami,* is not quite acquittal, but reprieve, and that's always worth taking.

Above all, don't believe your friends when they ask you to be sincere with them. They merely hope you will encourage them in the good opinion they have of themselves by providing them with the additional assurance they will find in your promise of sincerity. How could sincerity be a condition of friendship? A liking for truth at any cost is a passion that spares nothing and that nothing resists. It's a vice, at times a comfort, or a selfishness. Therefore, if you are in that situation, don't hesitate: promise to tell the truth and then lie as best you can. You will satisfy their hidden desire and doubly prove your affection.

This is so true that we rarely confide in those who are better than we. Rather, we are more in- clined to flee their society. Most often, on the other hand, we confess to those who are like us and who share our weaknesses. Hence we don't want to improve ourselves or be bettered, for we should first have to be judged in default. We merely wish to be pitied and encouraged in the course we have chosen. In short, we should like, at the same time, to cease being guilty and yet not to make the effort of cleansing ourselves. Not enough cynicism and not enough virtue. We lack the energy of evil as well as the energy of good. Do you know Dante? Really? The devil you say! Then you know that Dante accepts the idea of neutral angels in the quarrel between God and Satan. And he puts them in Limbo, a sort of vestibule of his Hell. We are in the vestibule, *cher ami.*

Patience? You are probably right. It would take patience to wait for the Last Judgment. But that's it, we're in a hurry. So much in a hurry, in deed, that I was obliged to make myself a judge-penitent. However, I first had to make shift with my discoveries and put myself right with my contemporaries' laughter. From the evening when I was called—for I was really called—I had to answer or at least seek an answer. It wasn't easy; for some time I floundered. To begin with, that perpetual laugh and the laughers had to teach me to see clearly within me and to discover at last that I was not simple. Don't smile; that truth is not so basic as it seems. What we call basic truths are simply the ones we discover after all the others.

However that may be, after prolonged research on myself, I brought out the fundamental duplicity of the human being. Then I realized, as a result of delving in my memory, that modesty helped me to shine, humility to conquer, and virtue to oppress. I used to wage war by peaceful means and eventually used to achieve, through disinterested means, everything I desired. For instance, I never complained that my birthday was overlooked; people were even surprised, with a touch of admiration, by my discretion on this subject. But the reason for my disinterestedness was even more discreet: I longed to be forgotten in order to be able to complain to myself. Several days before the famous date (which I knew very well) I was on the alert, eager to let nothing slip that might arouse the attention and memory of those on whose lapse I was counting (didn't I once go so far as to contemplate falsifying a friend's calendar?). Once my solitude was thoroughly proved, I could surrender to the charms of a virile self-pity.

Thus the surface of all my virtues had a less imposing reverse side. It is true that, in another sense, my shortcomings turned to my advantage. For example, the obligation I felt to conceal the vicious part of my life gave me a cold look that was confused with the look of virtue; my indifference made me loved; my selfishness wound up in my generosities. I stop there, for too great a symmetry would upset my argument. But after all, I presented a harsh exterior and yet could never resist the offer of a glass or of a woman! I was considered active, energetic, and my kingdom was the bed. I used to advertise my loyalty and I don't believe there is a single person I loved that I didn't eventually betray. Of course, my betrayals didn't stand in the way of my fidelity; I used to knock off a considerable pile of work through successive periods of idleness; and I had never ceased aiding my neighbor, thanks to my enjoyment in doing so. But however much I repeated such facts to myself, they gave me but superficial consolations. Certain mornings, I would get up the case against myself most thoroughly, coming to the conclusion that I excelled above all in scorn. The very people I helped most often were the most scorned. Courteously, with a solidarity charged with emotion, I used to spit daily in the face of all the blind.

Tell me frankly, is there any excuse for that? There is one, but so wretched that I cannot dream of advancing it. In any case, here it is: I have never been really able to believe that human affairs were serious matters. I had no idea where the serious might lie, except that it was not in all this I saw around me—which seemed to me merely an amusing game, or tiresome. There are really efforts and convictions I have never been able to understand. I always looked with amazement, and a certain suspicion, on those strange creatures who died for money, fell into despair over the loss of a "position," or sacrificed themselves with a high and mighty manner for the prosperity of their family. I could better understand that friend who had made up his mind to stop smoking and through sheer will power had succeeded. One morning he opened the paper, read that the first H- bomb had been exploded, learned about its wonderful effects, and hastened to a tobacco shop.

To be sure, I occasionally pretended to take life seriously. But very soon the frivolity of serious- ness struck me and I merely went on playing my role as well as I could. I played at being efficient, intelligent, virtuous, civic-minded, shocked, indulgent, fellow-spirited, edifying ... In short, there's no need of going on, you have already grasped that I was like my Dutchmen who are here without being here: I was absent at the moment when I took up the most space. I have never been really sincere and enthusiastic except when I used to indulge in sports, and in the army, when I used to act in plays we put on for our own amusement. In both cases there was a rule of the game, which was not serious but which we enjoyed taking as if it were. Even now, the Sunday matches in an over flowing stadium, and the theater, which I loved with the greatest passion, are the only places in the world where I feel innocent.

But who would consider such an attitude legitimate in the face of love, death, and the wages of the poor? Yet what can be done about it? I could imagine the love of Isolde only in novels or on the stage. At times people on their deathbed seemed to me convinced of their roles. The lines spoken by my poor clients always struck me as fitting the same pattern. Whence, living among men without sharing their interests, I could not manage to believe in the commitments I made. I was courteous and indolent enough to live up to what was expected of me in my profession, my family, or my civic life, but each time with a sort of indifference that spoiled everything. I lived my whole life under a double code, and my most serious acts were often the ones in which I was the least involved. Wasn't that after all the reason that, added to my blunders, I could not forgive myself, that made me revolt most violently against the judgment I felt forming, in me and around me, and that forced me to seek an escape?

For some time, my life continued outwardly as if nothing had changed I was on rails and speeding ahead As if purposely, people's praises increased. And that's just where the trouble came from. You remember the remark: "Woe to you when all men speak well of you!" Ah, the one who said that spoke words of wisdom! Woe to me! Consequently, the engine began to have whims, inexplicable breakdowns.

Then it was that the thought of death burst into my daily life. I would measure the years separating me from my end I would look for examples of men of my age who were already dead. And I was tormented by the thought that I might not have time to accomplish my task. What task? I had no idea. Frankly, was what I was doing worth continuing? But that was not quite it. A ridiculous fear pursued me, in fact: one could not die without having confessed all one's lies. Not to God or to one of his representatives; I was above that, as you well imagine. No, it was a matter of confessing to men, to a friend, to a beloved woman, for example. Otherwise, were there but one lie hidden in a life, death made it definitive. No one, ever again, would know the truth on this point, since the only one to know it was precisely the dead man sleeping on his secret. That absolute murder of a truth used to make me dizzy. Today, let me interject, it would cause me, instead, subtle joys. The idea, for instance, that I am the only one to know what everyone is looking for and that I have at home an object which kept the police of three countries on the run is a sheer delight. But let's not go into that. At the time, I had not yet found the recipe and I was fretting.

I pulled myself together, of course. What did one man's lie matter in the history of generations? And what pretension to want to drag out into the full light of truth a paltry fraud, lost in the sea of ages like a grain of sand in the ocean! I also told myself that the body's death, to judge from those I had seen, was in itself sufficient punishment that absolved all. Salvation was won (that is, the right to disappear definitively) in the sweat of the death agony. Nonetheless the discomfort grew; death was faithful at my bedside; I used to get up with it every morning, and compliments became more and more unbearable to me. It seemed to me that the falsehood increased with them so inordinately that never again could I put myself right.

A day came when I could bear it no longer. My first reaction was excessive. Since I was a liar, I would reveal this and hurl my duplicity in the face of all those imbeciles, even before they discovered it. Provoked to truth, I would accept the challenge. In order to forestall the laughter, I dreamed of hurling myself into the general derision. In short, it was still a question of dodging judgment. I wanted to put the laughers on my side, or at least to put myself on their side. I contemplated, for instance, jostling the blind on the street; and from the secret, unexpected joy this gave me I recognized how much a part of my soul loathed them; I planned to puncture the tires of invalids' vehicles, to go and shout "Lousy proletarian" under the scaffoldings on which laborers were working, to slap infants in the subway. I dreamed of all that and did none of it, or if I did something of the sort, I have forgotten it. In any case, the very word "justice" gave me strange fits of rage. I continued, of necessity, to use it in my speeches to the court. But I took my revenge by publicly inveighing against the humanitarian spirit; I announced the publication of a manifesto exposing the oppression that the oppressed inflict on decent people. One day while I was eating lobster at a sidewalk restaurant and a beggar bothered me, I called the proprietor to drive him away and loudly approved the words of that administrator of justice: "You are embarrassing people," he said. "Just put yourself in the place of these ladies and gents, after all!" Finally, I used to express, to whoever would listen, my regret that it was no longer possible to act like a certain Russian landowner whose character I admired. He would have a beating administered both to his peasants who bowed to him and to those who didn't bow to him in order to punish a boldness he considered equally impudent in both cases.

However, I recall more serious excesses. I began to write an *"Ode to the Police"* and an *"Apotheosis of the Guillotine."* Above all, I used to force myself to visit regularly the special cafés where our professional humanitarian free thinkers gathered. My good past record assured me of a welcome. There, without seeming to, I would let fly a forbidden expression: "Thank God ..." I would say, or more simply: "My God ..." You know what shy little children our café atheists are. A moment of amazement would follow that outrageous expression, they would look at one another dumbfounded, then the tumult would burst forth. Some would flee the café, others would gabble indignantly without listening to anything, and all would writhe in convulsions like the devil in holy water.

You must look on that as childish. Yet maybe there was a more serious reason for those little jokes. I wanted to upset the game and above all to destroy that flattering reputation, the thought of which threw me into a rage. "A man like you ..." people would say sweetly, and I would blanch. I didn't want their esteem because it wasn't general, and how could it be general, since I couldn't share it? Hence it was better to cover everything, judgment and esteem, with a cloak of ridicule. I had to liberate at all cost the feeling that was stifling me. In order to reveal to all eyes what he was made of, I wanted to break open the handsome wag-figure I presented everywhere. For instance, I recall an informal lecture I had to give to a group of young fledgling lawyers. Irritated by the fantastic praises of the president of the bar, who had introduced me, I couldn't resist long. I had begun with the enthusiasm and emotion expected of me, which I had no trouble summoning up on order. But I suddenly began to advise alliance as a system of defense. Not, I said, that alliance perfected by modern inquisitions which judge simultaneously a thief and an honest man in order to crush the second under the crimes of the first. On the contrary, I meant to defend the thief by exposing the crimes of the honest man, the lawyer in this instance. I explained myself very clearly on this point:

"Let us suppose that I have accepted the defense of some touching citizen, a murderer through jealousy. Gentlemen of the jury, consider, I should say, how venial it is to get angry when one sees one's natural goodness put to the test by the malignity of the fair sex. Is it not more serious, on the contrary, to be by chance on this side of the bar, on my own bench, without ever having been good or suffered from being duped? I am free, shielded from your severities, yet who am I? A Louis XIV in pride, a billy goat for lust, a Pharaoh for wrath, a king of laziness. I haven't killed anyone?

Not yet, to be sure! But have I not let deserving creatures die? Maybe. And maybe I am ready to do so again. Whereas this man—just look at him—will not do so again. He is still quite amazed to have accomplished what he has." This speech rather upset my young colleagues. After a moment, they made up their minds to laugh at it. They became completely reassured when I got to my conclusion, in which I invoked the human individual and his supposed rights. That day, habit won out.

By repeating these pleasant indiscretions, I merely succeeded in disconcerting opinion somewhat. Not in disarming it, or above all in disarming myself. The amazement I generally encountered in my listeners, their rather reticent embarrassment, somewhat like what you are showing—no, don't protest—did not calm me at all. You see, it is not enough to accuse yourself in order to clear yourself; otherwise, I'd be as innocent as a lamb. One must accuse oneself in a certain way, which it took me considerable time to perfect. I did not discover it until I fell into the most utterly forlorn state. Until then, the laughter continued to drift my way, without my random efforts succeeding in divesting it of its benevolent, almost tender quality that hurt me.

But the sea is rising, it seems to me. It won't be long before our boat leaves; the day is ending. Look, the doves are gathering up there. They are crowding against one another, hardly stirring, and the light is waning. Don't you think we should be silent to enjoy this rather sinister moment? No, I interest you? You are very polite. Moreover, I now run the risk of really interesting you. Before explaining myself on the subject of judges-penitent, I must talk to you of debauchery and of the little-ease.

V

You are wrong, *cher*, the boat is going at top speed. But the Zuider Zee is a dead sea, or almost. With its flat shores, lost in the fog, there's no saying where it begins or ends. So we are steaming along without any landmark; we can't gauge our speed We are making progress and yet nothing is changing. It's not navigation but dreaming.

In the Greek archipelago I had the contrary feeling. Constantly new islands would appear on the horizon. Their treeless backbone marked the limit of the sky and their rocky shore contrasted sharply with the sea. No confusion possible; in the sharp light everything was a landmark. And from one island to another, ceaselessly on our little boat, which was nevertheless dawdling, I felt as if we were scudding along, night and day, on the crest of the short, cool waves in a race full of spray and laughter. Since then, Greece itself drifts somewhere within me, on the edge of my memory, tirelessly ... Hold on, I, too, am drifting; I am becoming lyrical! Stop me, *cher,* I beg you.

By the way, do you know Greece? No? So much the better. What should we do there, I ask you? There one has to be pure in heart. Do you know that there male friends walk along the street in pairs holding hands? Yes, the women stay home and you often see a middle-aged, respectable man, sporting mustaches, gravely striding along the sidewalks, his fingers locked in those of his friend. In the Orient likewise, at times? All right. But tell me, would you take my hand in the streets of Paris? Oh, I'm joking. *We* have a sense of decorum; scum makes us stilted. Before appearing in the Greek islands, we should have to wash at length. There the air is chaste and sensual enjoyment as transparent as the sea. And we ...

Let's sit down on these steamer chairs. What a fog! I interrupted myself, I believe, on the way to the little-ease. Yes, I'll tell you what I mean. After having struggled, after having used up all my insolent airs, discouraged by the uselessness of my efforts, I made up my mind to leave the society of men. No, no, I didn't look for a desert island; there are no more. I simply took refuge among women. As you know, they don't really condemn any weakness; they would be more inclined to try to humiliate or disarm our strength. This is why woman is the reward, not of the warrior, but of the criminal. She is his harbor, his haven; it is in a woman's bed that he is generally arrested. Is she not all that remains to us of earthly paradise? In distress, I hastened to my natural harbor. But I no longer indulged in pretty speeches. I still gambled a little, out of habit; but invention was lacking. I hesitate to admit it for fear of using a few more naughty words: it seems to me that at that time I felt the need of love. Obscene, isn't it? In any case, I experienced a secret suffering, a sort of privation that made me emptier and allowed me, partly through obligation and partly out of curiosity, to make a few commitments. Inasmuch as I needed to love and be loved, I thought I was in love. In other words, I acted the fool.

I often caught myself asking a question which, as a man of experience, I had always previously avoided. I would hear myself asking: "Do you love me?" You know that it is customary to answer in such cases: "And you?" If I answered yes, I found myself committed beyond my real feelings. If I dared to say no, I ran the risk of ceasing to be loved, and I would suffer therefor. The greater the threat to the feeling in which I had hoped to find calm, the more I demanded that feeling of my partner. Hence I was led to ever more explicit promises and came to expect of my heart an ever more sweeping feeling. Thus I developed a deceptive passion for a charming fool of a woman who had so thoroughly read "true love" stories that she spoke of love with the assurance and conviction of an intellectual announcing the classless society. Such conviction, as you must know, is contagious. I tried myself out at tallying likewise of love and eventually convinced myself. At least until she became my mistress and I realized that the "true love" stories, though they taught how to talk of love, did not teach how to make love. After having loved a parrot, I had to go to bed with a serpent. So I looked elsewhere for the love promised by books, which I had never encountered in life.

But I lacked practice. For more than thirty years I had been in love exclusively with myself. What hope was there of losing such a habit? I didn't lose it and remained a trifler in passion. I multiplied the promises. I contracted simultaneous loves as, at an earlier period, I had multiple liaisons. In this way I piled up more misfortunes, for others, than at the time of my fine indifference. Have I told you that in despair my parrot wanted to let herself die of hunger? Fortunately I arrived in time and submitted to holding her hand until she met, on his return from a journey to Bali, the engineer with graying temples who had already been described to her by her favorite weekly. In any case, far from finding myself transported and absolved in the whirlwind—as the saying goes—of passion, I added even more to the weight of my crimes and to my deviation from virtue. As a result, I conceived such a loathing for love that for years I could not hear *"La Vie en rose"* or the *"Liebestod"* without gritting my teeth. I tried accordingly to give up women, in a certain way, and to live in a state of chastity. After all, their friendship ought to satisfy me. But this was tantamount to giving up gambling. Without desire, women bored me beyond all expectation, and obviously I bored them too. No more gambling and no more theater—I was probably in the realm of truth. But truth, *cher ami*, is a colossal bore.

Despairing of love and of chastity, I at last bethought myself of debauchery, a substitute for love, which quiets the laughter, restores silence, and above all, confers immortality. At a certain degree of lucid intoxication, lying late at night between two prostitutes and drained of all desire, hope ceases to be a torture, you see; the mind dominates the whole past, and the pain of living is over forever. In a sense, I had always lived in debauchery, never having ceased wanting to be immortal. Wasn't this the key to my nature and also a result of the great self-love I have told you about? Yes, I was bursting with a longing to be immortal. I was too much in love with myself not to want the precious object of my love never to disappear. Since, in the waking state and with a little self-knowledge, one can see no reason why immortality should be conferred on a salacious monkey, one has to obtain substitutes for that immortality. Because I longed for eternal life, I went to bed with harlots and drank for nights on end. In the morning, to be sure, my mouth was filled with the bitter taste of the mortal state. But, for hours on end, I had soared in bliss. Dare I admit it to you? I still remember with affection certain nights when I used to go to a sordid night club to meet a quick-change dancer who honored me with her favors and for whose reputation I even fought one evening with a bearded braggart. Every night I would strut at the bar, in the red light and dust of that earthly paradise, lying fantastically and drinking at length. I would wait for dawn and at last end up in the always unmade bed of my princess, who would indulge mechanically in sex and then sleep without transition. Day would come softly to throw light on this disaster and I would get up and stand motionless in a dawn of glory.

Alcohol and women provided me, I admit, the only solace of which I was worthy. I'll reveal this secret to you, *cher ami,* don't fear to make use of it. Then you'll see that true debauchery is liberating because it creates no obligations. In it you possess only yourself; hence it remains the favorite pastime of the great lovers of their own person. It is a jungle without past or future, without any promise above all, nor any immediate penalty. The places where it is practiced are separated from the world. On entering, one leaves behind fear and hope. Conversation is not obligatory there; what one comes for can be had without words, and often indeed without money. Ah, I beg you, let me pay honor to the unknown and forgotten women who helped me then! Even today, my recollection of them contains something resembling respect.

In any case, I freely took advantage of that liberation. I was even seen in a hotel dedicated to what is called sin, living simultaneously with a mature prostitute and an unmarried girl of the best society. I played the gallant with the first and gave the second an opportunity to learn the realities. Unfortunately the prostitute had a most middle-class nature; she since consented to write her memoirs for a confessions magazine quite open to modern ideas. The girl, for her part, got married to satisfy her unbridled instincts and make use of her remarkable gifts. I am not a little proud likewise to have been admitted as an equal, at that time, by a masculine guild too often reviled. But I'll not insist on that: you know that even very intelligent people glory in being able to empty one bottle more than the next man. I might ultimately have found peace and release in that happy dissipation. But, there too, I encountered an obstacle in myself. This time it was my liver, and a fatigue so dreadful that it hasn't yet left me. One plays at being immortal and after a few weeks one doesn't even know whether or not one can hang on till the next day.

The sole benefit of that experience, when I had given up my nocturnal exploits, was that life became less painful for me. The fatigue that was gnawing at my body had simultaneously cauterized many raw spots in me. Each excess decreases vitality, hence suffering. There is nothing frenzied about debauchery, contrary to what is thought. It is but a long sleep. You must have noticed that men who really suffer from jealousy have no more urgent desire than to go to bed with the woman they nevertheless think has betrayed them. Of course, they want to assure themselves once more that their dear treasure still belongs to them. They want to possess it, as the saying goes. But there is also the fact that immediately afterward they are less jealous. Physical jealousy is a result of the imagination at the same time that it is a self-judgment. One attributes to the rival the nasty thoughts one had oneself in the same circumstances. Fortunately excess of sensual satisfaction weakens both imagination and judgment. The suffering then lies dormant as long as virility does. For the same reasons adolescents lose their metaphysical unrest with their first mistress; and certain marriages, which are merely formalized debauches, become the monotonous hearses of daring and invention. Yes, *cher ami,* bourgeois marriage has put our country into slippers and will soon lead it to the gates of death.

I am exaggerating? No, but I am straying from the subject. I merely wanted to tell you the advantage I derived from those months of orgy. I lived in a sort of fog in which the laughter became so muffled that eventually I ceased to notice it. The indifference that already had such a hold over me now encountered no resistance and extended its sclerosis. No more emotions! An even temper, or rather no temper at all. Tubercular lungs are cured by drying up and gradually asphyxiate their happy owner. So it was with me as I peacefully died of my cure. I was still living on my work, although my reputation was seriously damaged by my flights of language and the regular exercise of my profession compromised by the disorder of my life. It is noteworthy, however, that I aroused less resentment by my nocturnal excesses than by my verbal provocations. The reference, purely verbal, that I often made to God in my speeches before the court awakened mistrust in my clients.

They probably feared that heaven could not represent their interests as well as a lawyer invincible when it came to the code of law. Whence it was but a step to conclude that I invoked the divinity in proportion to my ignorance. My clients took that step and became scarce. Now and then I still argued a case. At times even, forgetting that I no longer believed in what I was saying, I was a good advocate. My own voice would lead me on and I would follow it; without really soaring, as I once did, I at least got off the ground and did a little hedgehopping. Outside of my profession, I saw but few people and painfully kept alive one or two tired liaisons. It even happened that I would spend purely friendly evenings, without any element of desire, yet with the difference that, resigned to boredom, I scarcely listened to what was being said. I became a little fatter and at last was able to believe that the crisis was over. Nothing remained but to grow older.

One day, however, during a trip' to which I was treating a friend without telling her I was doing so to celebrate my cure, I was aboard an ocean liner—on the upper deck, of course. Suddenly, far off at sea, I perceived a black speck on the steel-gray ocean. I turned away at once and my heart began to beat wildly. When I forced myself to look, the black speck had disappeared. I was on the point of shouting, of stupidly calling for help, when I saw it again. It was one of those bits of refuse that ships leave behind them. Yet I had not been able to endure watching it; for I had thought at once of a drowning person. Then I realized, calmly as you resign yourself to an idea the truth of which you have long known, that that cry which had sounded over the Seine behind me years before had never ceased, carried by the river to the waters of the Channel, to travel throughout the world, across the limitless expanse of the ocean, and that it had waited for me there until the day I had encountered it. I realized likewise that it would continue to await me on seas and rivers, everywhere, in short, where lies the bitter water of my baptism. Here, too, by the way, aren't we on the water? On this flat, monotonous, interminable water whose limits are indistinguishable from those of the land? Is it credible that we shall ever reach Amsterdam? We shall never get out of this immense holy-water fount. Listen. Don't you hear the cries of invisible gulls? If they are crying in our direction, to what are they calling us?

But they are the same gulls that were crying, that were already calling over the Atlantic the day I realized definitively that I was not cured, that I was still cornered and that I had to make shift with it. Ended the glorious life, but ended also the frenzy and the convulsions. I had to submit and admit my guilt. I had to live in the little-ease. To be sure, you are not familiar with that dungeon cell that was called the little-ease in the Middle Ages. In general, one was forgotten there for life. That cell was distinguished from others by ingenious dimensions. It was not high enough to stand up in nor yet wide enough to lie down in. One had to take on an awkward manner and live on the diagonal; sleep was a collapse, and waking a squatting. *Mon cher,* there was genius—and I am weighing my words—in that so simple invention. Every day through the unchanging restriction that stiffened his body, the condemned man learned that he was guilty and that innocence consists in stretching joyously. Can you imagine in that cell a frequenter of summits and upper decks? What? One could live in those cells and still be innocent? Improbable! Highly improbable! Or else my reasoning would collapse. That innocence should be reduced to living hunchbacked—I refuse to entertain for a second such a hypothesis. Moreover, we cannot assert the innocence of anyone, whereas we can state with certainty the guilt of all. Every man testifies to the crime of all the others—that is my faith and my hope.

Believe me, religions are on the wrong track the moment they moralize and fulminate commandments. God is not needed to create guilt or to punish. Our fellow men suffice, aided by ourselves. You were speaking of the Last Judgment. Allow me to laugh respectfully. I shall wait for it resolutely, for I have known what is worse, the judgment of men. For them, no extenuating circumstances; even the good intention is ascribed to crime. Have you at least heard of the spitting cell, which a nation recently thought up to prove itself the greatest on earth? A walled-up box in which the prisoner can stand without moving. The solid door that locks him in his cement shell stops at chin level. Hence only his face is visible, and every passing jailer spits copiously on it. The prisoner, wedged into his cell, cannot wipe his face, though he is allowed, it is true, to close his eyes. Well, that, *mon cher,* is a human invention. They didn't need God for that little masterpiece.

What of it? Well, God's sole usefulness would be to guarantee innocence, and I am inclined to see religion rather as a huge laundering venture—as it was once but briefly, for exactly three years, and it wasn't called religion. Since then, soap has been lacking, our faces are dirty, and we wipe one another's noses. All dunces, all punished, let's all spit on one another and—hurry! to the little-ease! Each tries to spit first, that's all. I'll tell you a big secret, *mon cher*. Don't wait for the Last Judgment. It takes place every day.

No, it's nothing; I'm merely shivering a little in this damned humidity. We're landing anyway. Here we are. After you. But stay a little, I beg you, and walk home with me. I haven't finished; I must go on. Continuing is what is hard. Say, do you know why he was crucified—the one you are perhaps thinking of at this moment? Well, there were heaps of reasons for that. There are always reasons for murdering a man. On the contrary, it is impossible to justify his living. That's why crime always finds lawyers, and innocence only rarely. But, beside the reasons that have been very well explained to us for the past two thousand years, there was a major one for that terrible agony, and I don't know why it has been so carefully hidden. The real reason is that he knew *he* was not altogether innocent. If he did not bear the weight of the crime he was accused of, he had committed others—even though he didn't know which ones. Did he really not know them? He was at the source, after all; he must have heard of a certain Slaughter of the Innocents. The children of Judea massacred while his parents were taking him to a safe place—why did they die if not because of him? Those blood-spattered soldiers, those infants cut in two filled him with horror. But given the man he was, I am sure he could not forget them. And as for that sadness that can be felt in his every act, wasn't it the incurable melancholy of a man who heard night after night the voice of Rachel weeping for her children and refusing all comfort? The lamentation would rend the night, Rachel would call her children who had been killed for him, and he was still alive!

Knowing what he knew, familiar with everything about man—ah, who would have believed that crime consists less in making others die than in not dying oneself!—brought face to face day and night with his innocent crime, he found it too hard for him to hold on and continue. It was better to have done with it, not to defend himself, to die, in order not to be the only one to live, and to go elsewhere where perhaps he would be upheld. He was not upheld, he complained, and as a last straw, he was censored. Yes, it was the third evangelist, I believe, who first suppressed his complaint.

"Why hast thou forsaken me?"—it was a seditious cry, wasn't it? Well, then, the scissors! Mind you, if Luke had suppressed nothing, the matter would hardly have been noticed; in any case, it would not have assumed such importance. Thus the censor shouts aloud what he proscribes. The world's order likewise is ambiguous.

None the less, the censored one was unable to carry on. And I know, *cher,* whereof I speak. There was a time when I didn't at any minute have the slightest idea how I could reach the next one. Yes, one can wage war in this world, ape love, torture one's fellow man, or merely say evil of one's neighbor while knitting. But, in certain cases, carrying on, merely continuing, is superhuman. And he was not superhuman, you can take my word for it. He cried aloud his agony and that's why I love him, my friend who died without knowing.

The unfortunate thing is that he left us alone, to carry on, whatever happens, even when we are lodged in the little-ease, knowing in turn what he knew, but incapable of doing what he did and of dying like him. People naturally tried to get some help from his death. After all, it was a stroke of genius to tell us: "You're not a very pretty sight, that's certain! Well, we won't go into the details!

We'll just liquidate it all at once, on the cross!" But too many people now climb onto the cross merely to be seen from a greater distance, even if they have to trample somewhat on the one who has been there so long. Too many people have decided to do without generosity in order to practice charity. Oh, the injustice, the rank injustice that has been done him! It wrings my heart!

Good heavens, the habit has seized me again and I'm on the point of making a speech to the court. Forgive me and realize that I have my reasons. Why, a few streets from here there is a museum called Our Lord in the Attic. At the time, they had the catacombs in the attic. After all, the cellars are flooded here. But today—set your mind at rest—their Lord is neither in the attic nor in the cellar. They have hoisted him onto a judge's bench, in the secret of their hearts, and they smite, they judge above all, they judge in his name. He spoke softly to the adulteress: "Neither do I condemn thee!" but that doesn't matter; they condemn without absolving anyone. In the name of the Lord, here is what you deserve. Lord? He, my friend, didn't expect so much. He simply wanted to be loved, nothing more. Of course, there are those who love him, even among Christians. But they are not numerous. He had foreseen that too; he had a sense of humor. Peter, you know, the coward, Peter denied him: "I know not the man ... I know not what thou sayest ... etc." Really, he went too far! And my friend makes a play on words: "Thou art Peter, and upon this rock I will build my church." Irony could go no further, don't you think? But no, they still triumph! "You see, he had said it!" He had said it indeed; he knew the question thoroughly. And then he left forever, leaving them to judge and condemn, with pardon on their lips and the sentence in their hearts.

For it cannot be said there is no more pity; no, good Lord, we never stop talking of it. Simply, no one is ever acquitted any more. On dead innocence the judges swarm, the judges of all species, those of Christ and those of the Antichrist, who are the same anyway, reconciled in the little-ease. For one mustn't blame everything exclusively on the Christians. The others are involved too. Do you know what has become of one of the houses in this city that sheltered Descartes? A lunatic asylum. Yes, general delirium and persecution. We, too, naturally, are obliged to come to it. You have had a chance to observe that I spare nothing, and as for you, I know that you agree in thought. Wherefore, since we are all judges, we are all guilty before one another, all Christs in our mean manner, one by one crucified, always without knowing. We should be at least if I, Clamence, had not found a way out, the only solution, truth at last ...

No, I am stopping, *cher ami,* fear nothing! Besides, I'm going to leave you, for we are at my door. In solitude and when fatigued, one is after all inclined to take oneself for a prophet. When all is said and done, that's really what I am, having taken refuge in a desert of stones, fogs, and stagnant waters—an empty prophet for shabby times, Elijah without a messiah, choked with fever and alcohol, my back up against this moldy door, my finger raised toward a threatening sky, showering imprecations on lawless men who cannot endure any judgment. For they can't endure it, *très cher*, and that's the whole question. He who clings to a law does not fear the judgment that reinstates him in an order he believes in. But the keenest of human torments is to be judged without a law. Yet we are in that torment. Deprived of their natural curb, the judges, loosed at random, are racing through their job. Hence we have to try to go faster than they, don't we? And it's a real madhouse. Prophets and quacks multiply; they hasten to get there with a good law or a flawless organization before the world is deserted Fortunately, *I* arrived! I am the end and the beginning; I announce the law. In short, I am a judge-penitent.

Yes, yes, I'll tell you tomorrow what this noble profession consists of. You are leaving the day after tomorrow, so we are in a hurry. Come to my place, will you? Just ring three times. You are going back to Paris? Paris is far; Paris is beautiful; I haven't forgotten it. I remember its twilights at about this same season. Evening falls, dry and rustling, over the roofs blue with smoke, the city rumbles, the river seems to flow backward. Then I used to wander in the streets. They wander now too, I know! They wander, pretending to hasten toward the tired wife, the forbidding home ... Ah, mon ami, do you know what the solitary creature is like as he wanders in big cities? ...

VI

I'M EMBARASSED to be in bed when you arrive. It's nothing, just a little fever that I'm treating with gin. I'm accustomed to these attacks. Malaria, I think, that I caught at the time I was pope. No, I'm only half joking. I know what you're thinking: it's very hard to disentangle the true from the false in what I'm saying. I admit you are right. I myself ... You see, a person I knew used to divide human beings into three categories: those who prefer having nothing to hide rather than being obliged to lie, those who prefer lying to having nothing to hide, and finally those who like both lying and the hidden. I'll let you choose the pigeonhole that suits me.

But what do I care? Don't lies eventually lead to the truth? And don't all my stories, true or false, tend toward the same conclusion? Don't they all have the same meaning? So what does it matter whether they are true or false if, in both cases, they are significant of what I have been and of what I am? Sometimes it is easier to see clearly into the liar than into the man who tells the truth. Truth, like light, blinds. Falsehood, on the contrary, is a beautiful twilight that enhances every object.

Well, make of it what you will, but I was named pope in a prison camp.

Sit down, please. You are examining this room. Bare, to be sure, but clean. A Vermeer, without furniture or copper pots. Without books either, for I gave up reading some time ago. At one time, my house was full of half read books. That's just as disgusting as those people who cut a piece off a foie gras and have the rest thrown out. Anyway, I have ceased to like anything but confessions, and authors of confessions write especially to avoid confessing, to tell nothing of what they know. When they claim to get to the painful admissions, you have to watch out, for they are about to dress the corpse. Believe me, I know what I'm talking about. So I put a stop to it. No more books, no more useless objects either; the bare necessities, clean and polished like a coffin. Besides, these Dutch beds, so hard and with their immaculate sheets—one dies in them as if already wrapped in a shroud, embalmed in purity.

You are curious to know my pontifical adventures? Nothing out of the ordinary, you know. Shall I have the strength to tell you of them? Yes, the fever is going down. It was all so long ago. It was in Africa where, thanks to a certain Rommel, war was raging. I wasn't involved in it—no, don't worry. I had already dodged the one in Europe. Mobilized of course, but I never saw action. In a way, I regret it. Maybe that would have changed many things? The French army didn't need me on the front; it merely asked me to take part in the retreat. A little later I got back to Paris, and the Germans. I was tempted by the Resistance, about which people were beginning to talk just about the time I discovered that I was patriotic. You are smiling? You are wrong. I made my discovery on a subway platform, at the Châtelet station. A dog had strayed into the labyrinth of passageways. Big, wiry-haired, one ear cocked, eyes laughing, he was cavorting and sniffing the passing legs. I have a very old and very faithful attachment for dogs. I like them because they always forgive. I called this one, who hesitated, obviously won over, wagging his tail enthusiastically a few yards ahead of me. Just then, a young German soldier, who was walking briskly, passed me. Having reached the dog, he caressed the shaggy head. Without hesitating, the animal fell in step with the same enthusiasm and disappeared with him. From the resentment and the sort of rage I felt against the German soldier, it was dear to me that my reaction was patriotic. If the dog had followed a French civilian, I'd not even have thought of it. But, on the contrary, I imagined that friendly dog as the mascot of a German regiment and that made me fly into a rage. Hence the test was convincing.

I reached the Southern Zone with the intention of finding out about the Resistance. But once there and having found out, I hesitated. The under taking struck me as a little mad and, in a word, romantic. I think especially that underground action suited neither my temperament nor my preference for exposed heights. It seemed to me that I was being asked to do some weaving in a cellar, for days and nights on end, until some brutes should come to haul me from hiding, undo my weaving, and then drag me to another cellar to beat me to death. I admired those who indulged in such heroism of the depths, but couldn't imitate them.

So I crossed over to North Africa with the vague intention of getting to London. But in Africa the situation was not clear; the opposing parties seemed to be equally right and I stood aloof. I can see from your manner that I am skipping rather fast, in your opinion, over these details which have a certain significance. Well, let's say that, having judged you at your true value, I am skipping over them so that you will notice them the better. In any case, I eventually reached Tunisia, where a fond friend gave me work. That friend was a very intelligent woman who was involved in the movies. I followed her to Tunis and didn't discover her real business until the days following the Allied landing in Algeria. She was arrested that day by the Germans and I, too, but without having intended it. I don't know what became of her. As for me, no harm was done me and I realized, after considerable anguish, that it was chiefly as a security measure. I was interned near Tripoli in a camp where we suffered from thirst and destitution more than from brutality. I'll not describe it to you. We children of the mid-century don't need a diagram to imagine such places. A hundred and fifty years ago, people became sentimental about lakes and forests. Today we have the lyricism of the prison cell. Hence, I'll leave it to you. You need add but a few details: the heat, the vertical sun, the flies, the sand, the lack of water.

There was a young Frenchman with me who had faith. Yes, it's decidedly a fairy tale! The Du Guesclin type, if you will. He had crossed over from France into Spain to go and fight. The Catholic general had interned him, and having seen that in the Franco camps the chick-peas were, if I may say so, blessed by Rome, he had developed a profound melancholy. Neither the sky of Africa, where he had next landed, nor the leisures of the camp had distracted him from that melancholy. But his reflections, and the sun, too, had somewhat unhinged him. One day when, under a tent that seemed to drip molten lead, the ten or so of us were panting among the flies, he repeated his diatribes against the Roman, as he called him. He looked at us with a wild stare, his face unshaven for days. Bare to the waist and covered with sweat, he drummed with his hands on the visible keyboard of his ribs. He declared to us the need for a new pope who should live among the wretched instead of praying on a throne, and the sooner the better. He stared with wild eyes as he shook his head. "Yes," he repeated, "as soon as possible!" Then he calmed down suddenly and in a dull voice said that we must choose him among us, pick a complete man with his vices and virtues and swear allegiance to him, on the sole condition that he should agree to keep alive, in himself and in others, the community of our sufferings. "Who among us," he asked, "has the most failings?" As a joke, I raised my hand and was the only one to do so. "O.K., Jean-Baptiste will do." No, he didn't say just that because I had another name then. He declared at least that nominating oneself as I had done presupposed also the greatest virtue and proposed electing me. The others agreed, in fun, but with a trace of seriousness all the same. The truth is that Du Guesclin had impressed us. It seems to me that even I was not altogether laughing. To begin with, I considered that my little prophet was right; and then with the sun, the exhausting labor, the struggle for water, we were not up to snuff. In any case, I exercised my pontificate for several weeks, with increasing seriousness.

Of what did it consist? Well, I was something like a group leader or the secretary of a cell. The others, in any case, and even those who lacked faith, got into the habit of obeying me. Du Guesclin was suffering; I administered his suffering. I discovered then that it was not so easy as I thought to be a pope, and I remembered this just yesterday after having given you such a scornful speech on judges, our brothers. The big problem in the camp was the water allotment. Other groups, political or sectarian, had formed, and each prisoner favored his comrades. I was consequently led to favor mine, and this was a little concession to begin with. Even among us, I could not maintain complete equality. According to my comrades' condition, or the work they had to do, I gave an advantage to this or that one. Such distinctions are far-reaching, you can take my word for it. But decidedly I am tired and no longer want to think of that period. Let's just say that I closed the circle the day I drank the water of a dying comrade. No, no, it wasn't Du Guesclin; he was already dead, I believe, for he stinted himself too much. Besides, had he been there, out of love for him I'd have resisted longer, for I loved him—yes, I loved him, or so it seems to me. But I drank the water, that's certain, while convincing myself that the others needed me more than this fellow who was going to die anyway and that I had a duty to keep myself alive for them. Thus, *cher,* empires and churches are born under the sun of death. And in order to correct somewhat what I said yesterday, I am going to tell you the great idea that has come to me while telling all this, which—I'm not sure now—I may have lived or only dreamed. My great idea is that one must forgive the pope. To begin with, he needs it more than anyone else. Secondly, that's the only way to set oneself above him ...

Did you close the door thoroughly? Yes? Make sure, please. Forgive me, I have the bolt complex. On the point of going to sleep, I can never remember whether or not I pushed the bolt. And every night I must get up to verify. One can be sure of nothing, as I've told you. Don't think that this worry about the bolt is the reaction of a frightened possessor. Formerly I didn't lock my apartment or my car. I didn't lock up my money; I didn't cling to what I owned. To tell the truth, I was a little ashamed to own anything. Didn't I occasionally, in my social remarks, exclaim with conviction: "Property, gentlemen, is murder!" Not being sufficiently big-hearted to share my wealth with a deserving poor man, I left it at the disposal of possible thieves, hoping thus to correct injustice by chance. Today, moreover, I possess nothing. Hence I am not worried about my safety, but about myself and my presence of mind I am also eager to block the door of the closed little universe of which I am the king, the pope, and the judge.

By the way, will you please open that cupboard? Yes, look at that painting. Don't you recognize it? It is *"The Just Judges."* That doesn't make you jump? Can it be that your culture has gaps? Yet if you read the papers, you would recall the theft in 1934 m the St. Bavon Cathedral of Ghent, of one of the panels of the famous van Eyck altarpiece, *"The Adoration of the Lamb."* That panel was called *"The Just Judges."* It represented judges on horseback coming to adore the sacred animal. It was replaced by an excellent copy, for the original was never found. Well, here it is. No, I had nothing to do with it. A frequenter of *Mexico City* —you had a glimpse of him the other evening— sold it to the ape for a bottle, one drunken evening. I first advised our friend to hang it in a place of honor, and for a long time, while they were being looked for throughout the world, our devout judges sat enthroned at *Mexico City* above the drunks and pimps. Then the ape, at my request, put it in custody here. He balked a little at doing so, but he got a fright when I explained the matter to him. Since then, these estimable magistrates form my sole company. At *Mexico City*, above the bar, you saw what a void they left.

Why I did not return the panel? Ah! Ah! You have a policeman's reflex, you do! Well, I'll answer you as I would the state's attorney, if it could ever occur to anyone that this painting had wound up in my room. First, because it belongs not to me but to the proprietor of *Mexico City,* who deserves it as much as the Archbishop of Ghent. Secondly, because among all those who file by *"The Adoration. of the Lamb"* no one could distinguish the copy from the original and hence no one is wronged by my misconduct. Thirdly, because in this way I dominate. False judges are held up to the world's admiration and I alone know the true ones. Fourth, because I thus have a chance of being sent to prison—an attractive idea in a way. Fifth, because those judges are on their way to meet the Lamb, because there is no more lamb or innocence, and because the clever rascal who stole the panel was an instrument of the unknown justice that one ought not to thwart. Finally, because this way everything is in harmony. Justice being definitively separated from innocence—the latter on the cross and the former in the cupboard—I have the way clear to work according to my convictions. With a clear conscience I can practice the difficult profession of judge-penitent, in which I have set myself up after so many blighted hopes and contradictions; and now it is time, since you are leaving, for me to tell you what it is.

Allow me first to sit up so I can breathe more easily. Oh, how weak I am! Lock up my judges, please. As for the profession of judge-penitent, I am practicing it at present. Ordinarily, my offices are at *Mexico City*. But real vocations are carried beyond the place of work. Even in bed, even with a fever, I am functioning. Besides, one doesn't practice this profession, one breathes it constantly. Don't get the idea that I have talked to you at such length for five days just for the fun of it. No, I used to talk through my hat quite enough in the past. Now my words have a purpose. They have the purpose, obviously, of silencing the laughter, of avoiding judgment personally, though there is apparently no escape. Is not the great thing that stands in the way of our escaping it the fact that we are the first to condemn ourselves? Therefore it is essential to begin by extending the condemnation to all, without distinction, in order to thin it out at the start.

No excuses ever, for anyone; that's my principle at the outset. I deny the good intention, the respectable mistake, the indiscretion, the extenuating circumstance. With me there is no giving of absolution or blessing. Everything is simply totted up, and then: "It comes to so much. You are an evildoer, a satyr, a congenital liar, a homosexual, an artist, etc." Just like that. Just as flatly. In philosophy as in politics, I am for any theory that refuses to grant man innocence and for any practice that treats him as guilty. You see in me, *très cher,* an enlightened advocate of slavery.

Without slavery, as a matter of fact, there is no definitive solution. I very soon realized that. Once upon a time, I was always talking of freedom. At breakfast I used to spread it on my toast, I used to chew it all day long, and in company my breath was delightfully redolent of freedom. With that key word I would bludgeon whoever contradicted me; I made it serve my desires and my power. I used to whisper it in bed in the ear of my sleeping mates and it helped me to drop them I would slip it ...

Tchk! Tchk! I am getting excited and losing all sense of proportion. After all, I did on occasion make a more disinterested use of freedom and even—just imagine my naïveté—defended it two or three times without of course going so far as to die for it, but nevertheless taking a few risks. I must be forgiven such rash acts; I didn't know what I was doing. I didn't know that freedom is not a reward or a decoration that is celebrated with champagne. Nor yet a gift, a box of dainties designed to make you lick your chops. Oh, no! It's a chore, on the contrary, and a long-distance race, quite solitary and very exhausting. No champagne, no friends raising their glasses as they look at you affectionately. Alone in a forbidding room, alone in the prisoner's bog before the judges, and alone to decide in face of oneself or in the face of others' judgment. At the end of all freedom is a court sentence; that's why freedom is too heavy to bear, especially when you're down with a fever, or are distressed, or love nobody.

Ah, *mon cher*, for anyone who is alone, without God and without a master, the weight of days is dreadful. Hence one must choose a master, God being out of style. Besides, that word has lost its meaning; it's not worth the risk of shocking anyone. Take our moral philosophers, for instance, so serious, loving their neighbor and all the rest—nothing distinguishes them from Christians, except that they don't preach in churches. What, in your opinion, keeps them from becoming converted?

Respect perhaps, respect for men; yes, human respect. They don't want to start a scandal, so they keep their feelings to themselves. For example, I knew an atheistic novelist who used to pray every night. That didn't stop anything: how he gave it to God in his books! What a dusting off, as someone or other would say. A militant freethinker to whom I spoke of this raised his hands—with no evil intention, I assure you—to heaven: "You're telling me nothing new," that apostle sighed, "they are all like that." According to him, eighty per cent of our writers, if only they could avoid signing, would write and hail the name of God. But they sign, according to him, because they love themselves, and they hail nothing at all because they loathe themselves. Since, nevertheless, they cannot keep themselves from judging, they make up for it by moralizing. In short, their Satanism is virtuous. An odd epoch, indeed! It's not at all surprising that minds are confused and that one of my friends, an atheist when he was a model husband, got converted when he became an adulterer!

Ah, the little sneaks, play actors, hypocrites—and yet so touching! Believe me, they all are, even when they set fire to heaven. Whether they are atheists or churchgoers, Muscovites or Bostonians, all Christians from father to son. But it so happens that there is no more father, no more rule! They are free and hence have to shift for themselves; and since they don't want freedom or its judgments, they ask to be rapped on the knuckles, they invent dreadful rules, they rush out to build piles of faggots to replace churches. Savonarolas, I tell you. But they believe solely in sin, never in grace. They think of it, to be sure. Grace is what they want—acceptance, surrender, happiness, and maybe, for they are sentimental too, betrothal, the virginal bride, the upright man, the organ music.

Take me, for example, and I am not sentimental—do you know what I used to dream of? A total love of the whole heart and body, day and night, in an uninterrupted embrace, sensual enjoyment and mental excitement—all lasting five years and ending in death. Alas!

So, after all, for want of betrothal or uninterrupted love, it will be marriage, brutal marriage, with power and the whip.

The essential is that everything should become simple, as for the child, that every act should be ordered, that good and evil should be arbitrarily, hence obviously, pointed out.

And I agree, however Sicilian and Javanese I may be and not at all Christian, though I feel friendship for the first Christian of all. But on the bridges of Paris I, too, learned that I was afraid of freedom. So hurray for the master, whoever he may be, to take the place of heaven's law. "Our Father who art provisionally here ... Our guides, our delightfully severe masters, O cruel and beloved leaders ..." In short, you see, the essential is to cease being free and to obey, in repentance, a greater rogue than oneself. When we are all guilty, that will be democracy. Without counting, *cher ami*, that we must take revenge for having to die alone. Death is solitary, whereas slavery is collective. The others get theirs, too, and at the same time as we—that's what counts. All together at last, but on our knees and heads bowed.

Isn't it good likewise to live like the rest of the world, and for that doesn't the rest of the world have to be like me? Threat, dishonor, police are the sacraments of that resemblance. Scorned, hunted down, compelled, I can then show what I am worth, enjoy what I am, be natural at last. This is why, *très cher,* after having solemnly paid my respects to freedom, I decided on the sly that it had to be handed over without delay to anyone who comes along. And every time I can, I preach in my church of *Mexico City*, I invite the good people to submit to authority and humbly to solicit the comforts of slavery, even if I have to present it as true freedom.

But I'm not being crazy; I'm well aware that slavery is not immediately realizable. It will be one of the blessings of the future, that's all. In the meantime, I must get along with the present and seek at least a provisional solution. Hence I had to find another means of extending judgment to everybody in order to make it weigh less heavily on my own shoulders. I found the means. Open the window a little, please; it's frightfully hot. Not too much, for I am cold also. My idea is both simple and fertile. How to get everyone involved in order to have the right to sit calmly on the outside myself? Should I climb up to the pulpit, like many of my illustrious contemporaries, and curse humanity? Very dangerous, that is! One day, or one night, laughter bursts out without a warning. The judgment you are passing on others eventually snaps back in your face, causing some damage. And so what? you ask. Well, here's the stroke of genius. I discovered that while waiting for the masters with their rods, we should, like Copernicus, reverse the reasoning to win out. Inasmuch as one couldn't condemn others without immediately judging oneself, one had to overwhelm oneself to have the right to judge others. Inasmuch as every judge some day ends up as a penitent, one had to travel the road in the opposite direction and practice the profession of penitent to be able to end up as a judge. You follow me? Good. But to make myself even clearer, I'll tell you how I operate.

First I closed my law office, left Paris, traveled. I aimed to set up under another name in some place where I shouldn't lack for a practice. There are many in the world, but chance, convenience, irony, and also the necessity for a certain mortification made me choose a capital of waters and fogs, girdled by canals, particularly crowded, and visited by men from all corners of the earth. I set up my office in a bar in the sailors' quarter. The clientele of a port-town is varied. The poor don't go into the luxury districts, whereas eventually the gentlefolk always wind up at least once, as you have seen, in the disreputable places. I lie in wait particularly for the bourgeois, and the straying bourgeois at that; it's with him that I get my best results. Like a virtuoso with a rare violin, I draw my subtlest sounds from him.

So I have been practicing my useful profession at *Mexico City* for some time. It consists to begin with, as you know from experience, in indulging in public confession as often as possible. I accuse myself up and down. It's not hard, for I now have acquired a memory. But let me point out that I don't accuse myself crudely, beating my breast. No, I navigate skillfully, multiplying distinctions and digressions, too—in short, I adapt my words to my listener and lead him to go me one better. I mingle what concerns me and what concerns others. I choose the features we have in common, the experiences we have endured together, the failings we share—good form, in other words, the man of the hour as he is rife in me and in others. With all that I construct a portrait which is the image of all and of no one. A mask, in short, rather like those carnival masks which are both lifelike and stylized, so that they make people say: "Why, surely I've met him!" When the portrait is finished, as it is this evening, I show it with great sorrow: "This, alas, is what I am!" The prosecutor's charge is finished. But at the same time the portrait I hold out to my contemporaries becomes a mirror.

Covered with ashes, tearing my hair, my face scored by clawing, but with piercing eyes, I stand before all humanity recapitulating my shames without losing sight of the effect I am producing, and saying: "I was the lowest of the low." Then imperceptibly I pass from the "I" to the "we." When I get to "This is what we are," the trick has been played and I can tell them off. I am like them, to be sure; we are in the soup together. However, I have a superiority in that I know it and this gives me the right to speak. You see the advantage, I am sure. The more I accuse myself, the more I have a right to judge you. Even better, I provoke you into judging yourself, and this relieves me of that much of the burden. Ah, *mon cher*, we are odd, wretched creatures, and if we merely look back over our lives, there's no lack of occasions to amaze and horrify ourselves. Just try. I shall listen, you may be sure, to your own confession with a great feeling of fraternity.

Don't laugh! Yes, you are a difficult client; I saw that at once. But you'll come to it inevitably. Most of the others are more sentimental than intelligent; they are disconcerted at once. With the intelligent ones it takes time. It is enough to explain the method fully to them. They don't forget it; they reflect. Sooner or later, half as a game and half out of emotional upset, they give up and tell all. *You* are not only intelligent, you look polished by use. Admit, however, that today you feel less pleased with yourself than you felt five days ago? Now I shall wait for you to write me or come back. For you will come back, I am sure! You'll find me unchanged. And why should I change, since I have found the happiness that suits me? I have accepted duplicity instead of being upset about it. On the contrary, I have settled into it and found there the comfort I was looking for throughout life. I was wrong, after all, to tell you that the essential was to avoid judgment. The essential is being able to permit oneself everything, even if, from time to time, one has to profess vociferously one's own infamy. I permit myself everything again, and without the laughter this time. I haven't changed my way of life; I continue to love myself and to make use of others. Only, the confession of my crimes allows me to begin again lighter in heart and to taste a double enjoyment, first of my nature and secondly of a charming repentance.

Since finding my solution, I yield to everything, to women, to pride, to boredom, to resentment, and even to the fever that I feel delightfully rising at this moment. I dominate at last, but forever. Once more I have found a height to which I am the only one to climb and from which I can judge everybody. At long intervals, on a really beautiful night I occasionally hear a distant laugh and again I doubt. But quickly I crush everything, people and things, under the weight of my own infirmity, and at once I perk up.

So I shall await your respects at *Mexico City* as long as necessary. But remove this blanket; I want to breathe. You will come, won't you? I'll show you the details of my technique, for I feel a sort of affection for you. You will see me teaching them night after night that they are vile. This very evening, moreover, I shall resume. I can't do without it or deny myself those moments when one of them collapses, with the help of alcohol, and beats his breast. Then I grow taller, *très cher*, I grow taller, I breathe freely, I am on the mountain, the plain stretches before my eyes. How intoxicating to feel like God the Father and to hand out definitive testimonials of bad character and habits. I sit enthroned among my bad angels at the summit of the Dutch heaven and I watch ascending toward me, as they issue from the fogs and the water, the multitude of the Last Judgment.

They rise slowly; I already see the first of them arriving. On his bewildered face, half hidden by his hand, I read the melancholy of the common condition and the despair of not being able to escape it. And as for me, I pity without absolving,

I understand without forgiving, and above all, I feel at last that I am being adored!

Yes, I am moving about. How could I remain in bed like a good patient? I must be higher than you, and my thoughts lift me up. Such nights, or such mornings rather (for the fall occurs at dawn), I go out and walk briskly along the canals. In the livid sky the layers of feathers become thinner, the doves move a little higher, and above the roofs a rosy light announces a new day of my creation. On the Damrak the first streetcar sounds its bell in the damp air and marks the awakening of life at the extremity of this Europe where, at the same moment, hundreds of millions of men, my subjects, painfully slip out of bed, a bitter taste in their mouths, to go to a joyless work. Then, soaring over this whole continent which is under my sway without knowing it, drinking in the absinthe-colored light of breaking day, intoxicated with evil words, I am happy—I am happy, I tell you, I won't let you think I'm not happy, I am happy unto death! Oh, sun, beaches, and the islands in the path of the trade winds, youth whose memory drives one to despair!

I'm going back to bed; forgive me. I fear I got worked up; yet I'm not weeping. At times one wanders, doubting the facts, even when one has discovered the secrets of the good life. To be sure, my solution is not the ideal. But when you don't like your own life, when you know that you must change lives, you don't have any choice, do you? What can one do to become another? Impossible. One would have to cease being anyone, forget oneself for someone else, at least once. But how? Don't bear down too hard on me. I'm like that old beggar who wouldn't let go of my hand one day on a café terrace: "Oh, sir," he said, "it's not just that I'm no good, but you lose track of the light." Yes, we have lost track of the light, the mornings, the holy innocence of those who forgive themselves.

Look, it's snowing! Oh, I must go out! Amsterdam asleep in the white night, the dark jade canals under the little snow-covered bridges, the empty streets, my muted steps—there will be purity, even if fleeting, before tomorrow's mud. See the huge flakes drifting against the windowpanes. It must be the doves, surely. They finally make up their minds to come down, the little dears; they are covering the waters and the roofs with a thick layer of feathers; they are fluttering at every window. What an invasion! Let's hope they are bringing good news. Everyone will be saved, eh?—and not only the elect. Possessions and hardships will be shared and you, for example, from today on you will sleep every night on the ground for me. The whole shooting match, eh? Come now, admit that you would be flabbergasted if a chariot came down from heaven to carry me off, or if the snow suddenly caught fire. You don't believe it? Nor do I. But still I must go out.

All right, all right, I'll be quiet; don't get upset! Don't take my emotional outbursts or my ravings too seriously. They are controlled. Say, now that you are going to talk to me about yourself, I shall find out whether or not one of the objectives of my absorbing confession is achieved. I always hope, in fact, that my interlocutor will be a policeman and that he will arrest me for the theft of "*The Just Judges.*" For the rest—am I right?—no one can arrest me. But as for that theft, it falls within the provisions of the law and I have arranged everything so as to make myself an accomplice: I am harboring that painting and showing it to whoever wants to see it. You would arrest me then; that would be a good beginning. Perhaps the rest would be taken care of subsequently; I would be decapitated, for instance, and I'd have no more fear of death; I'd be saved. Above the gathered crowd, you would hold up my still warm head, so that they could recognize themselves in it and I could again dominate—an exemplar. All would be consummated; I should have brought to a close, unseen and unknown, my career as a false prophet crying in the wilderness and refusing to come forth.

But of course you are not a policeman; that would be too easy. What? Ah, I suspected as much, you see. That strange affection I felt for you had sense to it then. In Paris you practice the noble profession of lawyer! I sensed that we were of the same species. Are we not all alike, constantly talking and to no one, forever up against the same questions although we know the answers in advance? Then please tell me what happened to you one night on the quays of the Seine and how you managed never to risk your life. You yourself utter the words that for years have never ceased echoing through my nights and that I shall at last say through your mouth: "O young woman, throw yourself into the water again so that I may a second time have the chance of saving both of us!" A second time, eh, what a risky suggestion! Just suppose, *cher maître*, that we should be taken literally? We'd have to go through with it. Brr ...! The water's so cold! But let's not worry! It's too late now. It will always be too late. Fortunately!

THE END.